M000163916

Partners

DARTS FARM

FROBISHERS

HALLGARTEN
& NOVUM WINES

NOBLE ISLE

PKF
FRANCIS
CLARK
Shared Ambition

SALCOMBE GIN

Sharp's
BREWERY
ROCK · CORNWALL

SW660

TotalProduce

EDITOR
Jo Rees

EDITORIAL TEAM
Kathryn Lewis
Melissa Morris
Rosanna Rothery
Melissa Stewart
Selena Young

DESIGN
Christopher Mulholland

COMMERCIAL
Claire Fegan

PUBLISHING DIRECTOR
Tamsin Powell

PUBLISHING ASSISTANT
Charlotte Cummins

PUBLISHED BY
Salt Media
ideas@saltmedia.co.uk
01271 859299
saltmedia.co.uk

© 2022 Salt Media Ltd

The right of Salt Media to be identified as the author of
this work has been asserted by it in accordance with the
Copyright, Designs and Patents Act 1988.

A catalogue record of the book is available from the
British Library.

All rights reserved. No part of this publication may be
reproduced, distributed, or transmitted in any form or by
any means, including photocopying, recording, or other
electronic or mechanical methods, without the prior written
permission of the publisher, except in the case of brief
quotations embodied in critical reviews and certain other
non-commercial uses permitted by copyright law. For
permission requests, write to: Salt Media, 24 Castle Street,
Devon, EX31 1DR.

While every effort has been made to ensure the accuracy
of the information in this publication, we cannot be
held responsible for any errors or omissions and take no
responsibility for the consequences of error or for any loss
or damage suffered by users of any of the information
published on any of these pages. The views expressed
in this publication are not necessarily those of the
publisher or the editor.

We're serious about protecting the planet which is why
we print using solvent-free inks on FSC® certified paper,
working with a printer that holds ISO14001 certification for
environmental good practice.

MIX
Paper from
responsible sources
FSC® C010353

Escape to Trencherman's Country

Foreword

If you appreciate excellent food and drink and live in Trencherman's Country – that food-rich region of the UK from Cornwall to the Cotswolds – it's odds on you have a few local dining gems up your sleeve.

You know the places, those restaurants where cooking is top of the agenda and which you recommend to friends when they holiday nearby.

I always find myself urging out-of-area chums to visit my local hit list: The Farmers Arms in Woolsery for its astonishing own-grown produce, Pyne Arms on the edge of Exmoor for the unctuous beef suet pudding, and vibrant New Coast Kitchen in Croyde for smart cooking at the seaside.

'A hit list of insider's finds across the South West'

We've all got the inside info on quality restaurants near us but unfortunately, when we travel further afield, we're subject to trying to work out, via online reviews and websites, where's really good as opposed to where's good at marketing itself.

Consider *Trencherman's Guide* a hit list of insider's finds across the entire South West. Restaurants are only invited into the guide on meeting (and often surpassing) strict scoring criteria based on AA, *The Good Food Guide* and *Michelin Guide* ratings, along with grading visits by our experienced food journalists. Of course, not every restaurant makes the cut, which is why we're so confident about recommending those that do to our readers.

Trencherman's Guide has been published annually for 30 years, which is testament to its reputation for integrity in the hospitality industry. I hope this latest edition leads you to some new personal favourites.

Jo Rees
Editor

Contents

Welcome

Welcome to the *Trencherman's Guide*.

This 30th edition is a fantastic opportunity to look back at the progress that's been made in the South West dining scene over the last 30 years.

When the first *Trencherman's Guide* was published in 1992, just 25 restaurants hit the scoring criteria required to be a Trencherman's member and feature in the publication. The strict criteria haven't changed, but this 30th edition contains 116 restaurants, demonstrating the glut of excellent places, from Cornwall to the Cotswolds, where discerning diners can now eat out.

'It's no coincidence the South West hospitality scene is buzzing'

I think what's driven the success of the South West as one of UK's leading areas for restaurants and hospitality (and why people like to visit) is our connection with the produce grown and reared here. Our wonderful larder is one of the elements that differentiates the region.

We also have a fantastic food community and a wealth of talent – both chefs and service staff. And when you combine those with the natural beauty of the place, it's no coincidence the South West hospitality scene is buzzing.

Enjoy using the Guide – I hope you have some amazing experiences.

Michael Caines MBE
Chairman of the Trencherman's committee

Trencherman's at

For three decades, the *Trencherman's Guide* has charted the rise of the South West dining scene. We talk to Kit Chapman and Michael Caines about its inception and future, and mark its 30th birthday with images from events in recent Trencherman's history

The Seafood Restaurant, 2011

Kit Chapman

The first *Trencherman's Guide*

Since it was launched in 1992 by Kit Chapman of The Castle at Taunton and Paul Henderson formerly of Gidleigh Park in Devon, the *Trencherman's Guide* has documented the development of the unique food and dining culture of the South West of England.

During the Guide's 30-year history, it's chronicled restaurants as they've launched and closed, and marked food trends as they've bubbled up and then popped, never to be seen again. It's also witnessed established restaurants such as The Angel in Dartmouth as they pass from one generation of remarkable chefs to the next.

'Challenges, changes and opportunities span from the introduction of nouvelle cuisine to the rise of smart dining pubs'

Changes, challenges and opportunities within the industry during the last three decades span from the introduction of nouvelle cuisine to the rise of smart dining pubs. They've included the craft drinks boom, the noughties' food revolution, online booking and websites, recessions, Covid-19 and Brexit. The *Trencherman's Guide* has marked each moment and reflected the region's food and hospitality industry while helping diners discover superb restaurants.

Lucknam Park Hotel & Spa, 2012

Michael Caines

The Seafood Restaurant, 2011

Kit Chapman explains how the guide began:
'*I was very good friends with Paul Henderson who, in 1977, bought and ran Gidleigh Park. During the 1980s we could both see it was becoming a golden age for the restaurant trade. Suddenly, eating out became very fashionable and young British chefs were learning how to cook really well from luminaries like the Roux brothers, Raymond Blanc and Anton Mosimann.*'

Alongside talented foreign chefs teaching young Brits, there were a number of factors that also contributed to that golden moment. Kit says:

'*One was the introduction of colour supplements in the newspapers which made food look very sexy. There were also a lot of television cooks coming on screen – this was post Fanny Cradock – and it all became quite serious. Then Francis Coulson opened Sharrow Bay in Cumbria, and that was the start of the rise and rise of the English country house hotel.*'

'The introduction of colour supplements in the newspapers made food look very sexy'

Kit and Paul knew something interesting was emerging and wanted to be part of it.

'*Paul and I thought this was all very exciting,*' he says. '*We already had a Michelin star at The Castle, and he had one at Gidleigh Park, but we wanted to focus on bringing what was happening around the country – and in London in particular – to the West Country.*'

The Manor House, 2013

Southernhay House Hotel, 2014

Watergate Bay Hotel, 2014

20

They also wanted to show the rest of the UK what was going on in the region, and this led to the idea of creating a dining guide. It wasn't going to be any old roundup of eateries, however. Kit says: 'We wanted to control who went in so we could only showcase the best restaurants in the South West of England.

'We constructed a fairly simple and fair scoring system (which is still the basis of the one used now). We needed a system as we didn't have the time to become restaurant inspectors. The scoring was based on three guidebooks: the Michelin Guide, The Good Food Guide and the AA Guide. We adopted a points system based on those guides and applied it to the restaurants.'

'We wanted to focus on bringing what was happening in London to the West Country'

The pair roped in the West Country Tourist Board (which later became South West Tourism) to publish it.

'The idea was that the restaurants in the guide would display it in their premises and we'd therefore encourage cross-referrals, creating a community of people interested in food and drink who would know where the really great restaurants were to be found.

The Manor House, 2015

The Seafood Restaurant, 2016

Harvey Nichols, 2016

Lympstone Manor, 2018

'We introduced a launch lunch for each annual edition, which was held at different Trencherman's restaurants. We hosted a few events at The Castle and it was also held at some of the other hotels and bigger restaurants such as Rick and Jill Stein's The Seafood Restaurant. It was wonderful and a great communal thing among the restaurateurs in the South West. And so it is today.'

His thoughts on the guide, 30 years on? 'I have to say hats off to Michael [Caines]. I'm so pleased he took it on with such enthusiasm and energy; he deserves great credit for that. Otherwise, the thing might have just died away, but it's still here and thriving.'

'We introduced a launch lunch for each annual edition, which was held at different Trencherman's restaurants'

Trencherman's chairman Michael Caines of Lympstone Manor got involved with the Guide while he was head chef of Gidleigh Park, where he held two Michelin stars for 18 consecutive years. When South West Tourism, which published the guide, was axed as a result of government cuts in 2011, Michael secured the future of the Guide with Devon publishing company Salt Media.

Lympstone Manor, 2018

Salcombe Harbour Hotel, 2018

Lucknam Park Hotel & Spa, 2018

He's been chairman of the Trencherman's committee for over a decade and, along with fellow high-profile chefs such as Paul Ainsworth, Rick Stein and Nathan Outlaw, has helped bring the South West hospitality scene to a wider national and international audience.

How does he think we can ensure another 30 years of hospitality excellence in the South West?

'We need to think about how we can continue to attract people to the South West – not just to come and eat here, but also to come and live here,' says Michael.

'The situation is so challenging that some restaurants are currently unable to open full time'

'That means investing in the right infrastructure and an educational structure which will attract and develop young people in the industry.'

The chef is referring to the difficulties that restaurants are experiencing in recruiting people to work in both kitchens and front of house. The situation is so challenging that some restaurants are currently unable to open full time.

Calcot & Spa, 2019

The Seafood Restaurant, 2020

Saunton Sands Hotel, 2019

The Alverton Hotel, 2022

26

'*A lot has been achieved in 30 years, but now I think we need to turn our attention to the welfare of our hospitality staff because that's essential.*'

However, it's not all doom and gloom, as the number of high calibre restaurants in the 30th edition testifies.

Michael also sees green shoots of opportunity for the industry in areas which are revealing themselves as possible avenues out of challenging times. One example is the changing climate, which is making it possible to grow grapes in the South West in a way that was unheard of until recently. Michael has planted vines in the grounds of Lympstone Manor and says: '*The emergence of vineyards and viniculture in this part of the country is very exciting and will, I think, become part of our tourism offer as well as our food culture.*

'The South West is a place of outstanding natural beauty and that's a huge asset which will help us lock into green tourism'

'*That ties in to the essential work that needs to be done to create sustainable businesses and protect biodiversity in our natural environment. The South West is a place of outstanding natural beauty and that's a huge asset which will help us lock into green tourism.*' He's confident about the future and asserts: '*Opportunities like that will help keep the South West on the map and the hospitality industry thriving.*'

More ways to escape to Trencherman's Country

Second helpings

Get a second helping of the *Trencherman's Guide* via the regular email newsletter which provides the low-down on new events and openings, features interviews with chefs and reveals great places to eat out via seasonally themed curations.

You'll also get advance notification of voting for the annual Trencherman's Awards.

Sign up for the newsletter at
trenchermans-guide.com/ join-the-club

Digital Trencherman's

Want to browse more images of the restaurants in the Guide? Or left your copy of the *Trencherman's Guide* at home and need a dining recommendation on the hoof? The Trencherman's website ensures you're only ever a few clicks away from finding the best places to eat out in the South West.

trenchermans-guide.com

Be social

Stay up-to-date with the latest foodie news via the Trencherman's social channels.

f The Trenchermans Guide

𝕏 @trenchermans

◎ @trenchermans_guide

TRENCHERMAN'S

Awards
22

The South West's culinary stars were crowned at the annual Trencherman's Awards, which took place in March 2022 at The Alverton Hotel in Truro.

Trencherman's Guide readers cast over 20,000 votes to determine who would take the gongs – and here they are. You'll also find the winners highlighted throughout the Guide.

Award for Special Contribution
Mark Dodson of The Masons Arms | 47

Award for Creativity and Innovation
Sponsored by Sharp's Brewery

Winner: **The Idle Rocks**

Finalists: Kota Restaurant,
Outlaw's New Road, THE PIG–at Combe

Award for Special Contribution
Sponsored by PKF Francis Clark

Winner: **Mark Dodson of The Masons Arms**

Finalists: Elly Wentworth of The Angel –
Taste of Devon, Mark Hix of The Oyster &
Fish House, Laurence & Helen Beere of
The Olive Tree Restaurant

Best Trencherman's Restaurant
Sponsored by Total Produce

Winner: **Porthminster Beach Cafe**

Finalists: Puro, Salumi Bar & Eatery,
The Masons Arms

Best Trencherman's Hotel
Sponsored by Noble Isle

Winner: **Two Bridges Hotel**

Finalists: Lucknam Park Hotel & Spa,
The Greenbank Hotel, THE PIG – near Bath

Best Trencherman's Chef
Sponsored by Hallgarten & Novum Wines

Winner: **Chris Cleghorn of The Olive Tree Restaurant**

Finalists: Elly Wentworth of The Angel –
Taste of Devon, Hywel Jones of Lucknam Park
Hotel & Spa, Matthew Beardshall of Wilder

Best Trencherman's Pub

Winner: **The Fox Inn**

Finalists: Acorn Inn, The Barley Sheaf,
The Dartmoor Inn

Best Front of House Team

Winner: **THE PIG–at Harlyn Bay**

Finalists: Acorn Inn, The Alverton Hotel,
Tom's Lyme Regis

Best Bar List

Winner: **Fistral Beach Hotel and Spa**

Finalists: The Greenbank Hotel,
The Longstore, Fletcher's Restaurant

Best Newcomer

Winner: **Three Horseshoes Pub & Kitchen**

Finalists: Pattard Restaurant,
Candlelight Inn, Tom's Lyme Regis

How to
use the
guide

Restaurants are invited into the guide on surpassing strict scoring criteria, so you can be confident they deliver a seriously good dining experience.

To make the guide easy to use, the restaurants are divided into geographical regions. Each restaurant has a number, which you'll also find on the map at the beginning of the chapter for that region.

Look for these symbols throughout the guide:

Restaurants that achieve an exceptionally high score are identified as Higher Members via this symbol

Restaurants where you can stay the night are identified using this symbol

Trencherman's Awards 2022 winners are also highlighted throughout the guide using this symbol

Gloucestershire
& Oxfordshire

Restaurants listed in the guide correspond to the numbers plotted on the map.

All locations are approximate

1 Broadway

3

2 Lower Slaughter

7

CHELTENHAM

GLOUCESTER

Shipton-under-Wychwood

Minster Lovell

4

Stroud

6

Nailsworth

Cirencester

5

1 Buckland Manor

Elegant country house hospitality

Near Broadway, Worcestershire, WR12 7LY **01386 852626**

bucklandmanor.co.uk

A stay at Buckland Manor is like visiting the home of good friends, albeit chums who are exceptional hosts and primed to pamper you with afternoon tea on a whim, ply you with fine tipples before dinner, suggest on-point wine pairings and won't mind a jot if you have a long lie-in before breakfast.

That's because the warm reception to be found at this English manor house, a member of the Andrew Brownsword Hotels collection, is an integral part of its elegant country house appeal. Tucked away in a tranquil corner of the Cotswold village of Buckland amid ten acres of grounds, it's the very definition of timeless tranquillity.

At the heart of this impeccable hospitality are award-winning menus crafted by head chef Mark Potts. Along with his hardworking team, he provides guests with a memorable culinary experience which stays true to its Cotswold location. Fresh local produce from the neighbouring Vale of Evesham and herbs from Buckland Manor's grounds are crafted into modern and innovative British dishes.

A starter of rabbit leg cannelloni with mustard, radish and turnip might be followed by mains such as free-range chicken breast with stuffed thigh, wild garlic and sweetcorn. The gourmet adventures are matched by a magnificent wine cellar which provides a broad range of potential pairings for each course.

Trencherman's tip: those tempted to explore the Manor's delights in greater depth can book a stay at one of its 15 quintessentially English country-house guestrooms.

Chef Mark Potts | **3 course dinner from** £85
Seats 44 | **Bedrooms** 15 | **Room rate from** £310

2 The Slaughters Manor House

Artful dining in the Cotswold countryside

Copsehill Road, Lower Slaughter, Gloucestershire, GL54 2HP **01451 820456**

slaughtersmanor.co.uk

This beautiful 17th-century manor house in the heart of a Cotswold village combines authentic tradition with creative modernity.

Dine in the contemporary orangery-style restaurant amid crisp white table linen and the original stonework of the open fireplace and feast on head chef Nik Chappell's artful creations.

Nik and team use their menus to celebrate the finest Cotswold produce, and mix up the use of regionally farmed and reared ingredients with foraged finds from the surrounding countryside.

The incredible edibles can be paired with some special delights from a strong wine list which is expertly curated by the house sommelier.

Guests can also explore the wines, and pre-dinner cocktails, at the elegant bar which provides the opportunity to perch on a blush-pink bar stool and watch the concoctions being crafted.

Lunch, dinner and afternoon tea are all pleasures to be experienced, the latter a wonderful way to combine an English tradition with a wander around the elegant gardens.

Chef Nik Chappell | **3 course dinner from** £80
Seats 25 | **Bedrooms** 19 | **Room rate from** £285

3 Restaurant GL50

Eco-friendly excellence in Cheltenham

8 Norfolk House, Chester Walk, Cheltenham, Gloucestershire, GL50 3JX **01242 228555**
restaurantgl50.com

Restaurant GL50 chef-patron Jonas Lodge's exceptional credentials go beyond being Raymond Blanc-trained. He also worked under Heston Blumenthal and Paul Heathcote, maintained two AA rosettes and won AA Pub of the Year as head chef of The Bell at Ramsbury before opening his own restaurant in Cheltenham.

With just 35 covers, this is an intimate experience and Jonas' commitment to minimising waste (by using every bit of the British ingredients he's sourced) also makes it a very contemporary one.

The chef focuses on buying only whole fish and large cuts of meat, which he utilises in their entirety so nothing ends up in the bin.

From an environmental standpoint, it's the future of restaurant cooking.

Feast on innovative dishes such as glazed rose veal with barbecued asparagus, seaweed hollandaise and black garlic, and salted caramel beef-fat tart with cranberry, pecan and potato ice cream, served in a crisp modern environment where nothing is too much trouble. If you're feeling adventurous, call ahead and ask for the surprise tasting experience – at the end of the meal you'll receive a copy of the bespoke menu.

Unique house cocktails and wine recommendations are on-point and there's a pairing option if you plump for the tasting menu.

Chef Jonas Lodge | **3 course dinner from** £45 | **Seats** 35

4 The Bell Inn

Award-winning Cotswold inn

Bell Lane, Selsley, Gloucestershire, GL5 5JY **01453 753801**

thebellinnselsley.com

Dog-owning gourmets and gin-ophiles should bookmark this 16th-century Cotswold inn, as The Bell Inn's fido-friendly policy and collection of 80 gins make it an unusual find.

An even greater reason to visit is chef owner Mark Payne's cooking, which is big on seasonal and local produce, including veggies from his own allotment and lamb from the fields next door. Everything is treated with the greatest respect: humble blade of beef, for example, is gently cooked for five hours until it falls apart under the merest application of knife and fork.

Starters such as smoked haddock and dill rillettes – fresh, lemony, lightly dressed and served with crisp sourdough toast – provide another example of simple things done extremely well.

If, after two courses you're thinking of swerving pud, take the middle ground and order the house Gingato – a scoop of homemade vanilla ice cream drenched, affogato style, in rhubarb and ginger gin liqueur.

Trencherman's tip: three smart guestrooms – also dog-friendly – are to be found above the inn.

Chef Mark Payne | **3 course dinner from** £32
Seats 58 | **Bedrooms** 3 | **Room rate from** £90

5 Wilder

Culinary theatre in Nailsworth

3 Market Street, Nailsworth, Gloucestershire, GL6 0BX **01453 835483**
wild-garlic.co.uk

Curious diners can't sneak an online peek at the latest menu ahead of their evening at Wilder. Chef patron Matthew Beardshall likes to keep guests on the edge of their seats, so details of each course of the tasting menu are only unveiled as the dish reaches the table. The result is suspense and theatre.

Only the finest locally sourced ingredients earn a place in Matthew's expertly executed dishes and the three AA rosette eight-course dining experience takes guests on a journey of texture, colour and flavour.

Gourmets can amplify the experience further by opting for the accompanying wine flight of noteworthy finds from some of the world's finest vineyards. There's also an alternative non-alcoholic line-up of interesting tipples.

Turn your trip into a gastronomic getaway by staying at Cotswold-chic sister property Wild Garlic Rooms across the road. The two newly refurbished self-catering apartments, plus collection of five cosy bedrooms, are the perfect base from which to explore Nailsworth and beyond.

Chef Matthew Beardshall | **8 course dinner** £95 | **Seats** 18
Bedrooms 7 | **Room rate from** £90

6 Minster Mill

Oxfordshire dining oasis

Minster Lovell, Oxfordshire, OX29 0RN **01993 774441**
minstermill.co.uk

Just a short drive from the dreaming spires of Oxford stands glamorous Cotswold retreat Minster Mill, part of the Andrew Brownsword Hotels collection.

Set in glorious grounds, the honey-coloured converted mill is a rural idyll in the village of Minster Lovell. Charming Cotswold-stone buildings and barns are flanked by 65 acres of enchanting riverside gardens.

Start any visit with a classic cocktail in the lofty gallery bar or head to the garden terrace to sip while surrounded by wildflower meadows, woodland and the burble of the River Windrush.

Dinner is served beneath the vaulted ceilings and oak beams of the three AA rosette restaurant where head chef Joshua Brimmell specialises in contemporary British cooking. Creative flair and a commitment to supporting regional producers sees each artfully devised dish fused with a local twist. Wine and Champagne from the extensive Brownsword cellar complete the experience.

The hotel isn't just a picturesque dinner destination, of course. Drop by to enjoy the lunch menu or the Laurent-Perrier Champagne afternoon tea with freshly baked scones, cakes and pastries.

Sleek streamlined Scandi-style bedrooms, a garden spa and traditional amusements such as croquet and tennis are enticements to stay longer.

Trencherman's tip: with its flagstone floors and inglenook fireplaces, sister property The Old Swan, across the road, provides the more casual pleasures of a hand-raised pie and glass of cool ale.

Chef Joshua Brimmell | **3 course dinner from** £70
Seats 25 | **Bedrooms** 38 | **Room rate from** £225

DARTS FARM
growing the passion

dartsfarm.co.uk

7 The Wychwood Inn

Crowd-pleasing pub dining

High Street, Shipton-under-Wychwood, Chipping Norton, Oxfordshire, OX7 6BA **01993 831185**
thewychwoodinn.com

The Cotswolds is the spiritual home of the cosy dining pub – and The Wychwood Inn a fine example of type.

Head chef Joe McCarthy honours the Shipton-under-Wychwood inn's heritage with a menu of quality modern British dishes, adding bespoke contemporary touches via precise plating and creative interventions.

Tried-and-tested classics, such as chicken kiev made with garlic and parsley cultured butter or The Wychwood burger served with coleslaw and skin-on fries, are the kind of dishes you could revisit every week, so it's no surprise they're menu stalwarts.

A new heated and covered dining area in the spacious garden offers alfresco drinking and dining year-round (well-behaved dogs are welcome), so this is a fabulous spot for a post-walk pint and plate of beer-battered fish and chips.

Five comfortable guestrooms above the inn, good cooking, an atmospheric interior and lush countryside gives The Wychwood all the credentials required for an excellent weekend away in rural Oxfordshire.

Trencherman's tip: special occasion coming up? Book one of the private dining rooms.

Chef Joe McCarthy | **3 course dinner from** £35
Seats 84 | **Bedrooms** 5 | **Room rate from** £108

**Restaurants listed in the guide
correspond to the numbers plotted
on the map.**

All locations are approximate

SWINDON

Castle Combe

Colerne

Lacock

BATH

Bradford-on-Avon

East Chisenbury

8 Luncknam Park Hotel & Spa

Elegant escapism near Bath

Colerne, Wiltshire, SN14 8AZ **01225 742777**
lucknampark.co.uk

Wind your way up the tree-lined driveway that runs through the 500 acres surrounding Lucknam Park to discover one of England's most astonishingly beautiful country house hotels.

Elegance is the watchword at this Palladian mansion, yet the experience isn't pretentious. Contemporary elements such as the luxury spa and a relaxed brasserie provide an alternative to the decadent dining experience at Restaurant Hywel Jones.

The latter is the reason Lucknam has retained a Michelin star for 17 consecutive years and why gourmets flock to this Wiltshire gem. And the best way to explore Hywel's culinary prowess is to plump for his seasonal tasting menu.

Any dining occasion at the hotel should start with cocktails in the drawing room where you can lose yourself in the beautiful objets d'art, sumptuous furnishings and views over the manicured gardens before taking a seat in the dining room.

For a casual lunch (or a laid-back supper after an afternoon in the spa), the contemporary Brasserie offers wood-fired delights such as roast Cornish hake with capers, brown shrimps, lemon and parsley, and puds like Bramley apple-crumble tart with rum and raisin custard. When the weather's good, huge bi-fold windows open to create an alfresco dining vibe which befits the garden setting.

Trencherman's tip: Lucknam is just a short drive from the city of Bath, providing a wonderful escape after a day of sightseeing.

Chef Hywel Jones | **3 course dinner from** £55 (at Brasserie)
Seats 66, plus 44 in Brasserie | **Bedrooms** 43, plus 6 cottages | **Room rate from** £400

9 The Bunch of Grapes

New-wave pub dining

14 Silver Street, Bradford-on-Avon, Wiltshire, BA15 1JY **01225 938088**
thebunchofgrapes.com

A rural village pub may be the unlikely setting for cutting-edge cooking, but it's where Tony Casey crafts intriguing compilations which play with flavour, texture and style. The talented chef skippered kitchens in Bath and Bristol before taking over The Bunch of Grapes in 2018, and the cities' losses have been Bradford-on-Avon's gain.

Kick off your visit with cocktails as you ponder the difficult choice laid before you: should you pick what you fancy and go à la carte, or throw caution to the wind and plump for the tasting menu? Either way, top-quality ingredients take centre stage in standout dishes such as brill with cockles, coconut broth, shiitake and pak choi, and puds such as mascarpone mousse with miso ice cream, meringue and strawberry yogurt.

If you're looking for something more casual, there's also a bar menu which features the likes of salt and pepper squid, breaded chicken burger with garlic mayo and cheddar, and cauliflower and truffle risotto. Whatever you order, keep your phone nearby so you can snap a photo before you dig in – Tony's dishes are as pleasing to admire as they are to devour.

The interior styling of the ancient pub is equally photogenic: tables centre around an imposing bar featuring an impressive collection of spirits and glassware. On the first floor, striking blue walls and produce-themed artwork set the scene for the eye-catching dishes.

Chef Tony Casey | **3 course dinner from** £32.50 | **Seats** 60

FROBISHERS

Frobishers are experts in unique and flavoursome soft drinks. With 30 years' experience of sourcing delicious fruit and the best botanicals from around the world, they know how to make the perfect tipple!

10 Red Lion Freehouse

Creative cooking with wow factor

East Chisenbury, Pewsey, Wiltshire, SN9 6AQ **01980 671124**
redlionfreehouse.com

Picture all the charms of a country pub – thatched roof, flagstones, locals at the bar, real ales on tap and a warm welcome – and combine them with the prowess of two talented chef owners who craft restaurant dishes with wow factor, and it's little surprise this family-run local has won a raft of foodie accolades and become a sought-out dining destination.

Everything at this village pub near Salisbury Plain is crafted with superb attention to detail, from the pub-snack scotch eggs to the sumptuous tasting menu. If something can be made in-house, it is. If not, owners Brittany and Guy Manning will source it from top-notch producers.

Dishes such as wild brill with samphire, Shetland mussels, garden potatoes, dill and langoustine bisque showcase Guy's superb creativity. Pastry chef Brittany's formidable skills come to the fore in the likes of raspberry sorbet with wasabi, lime curd and zested shortbread.

Guests can dine inside to imbibe the rustic ambience or, on a warm day, take advantage of the garden tables. The à la carte menu with wine pairings includes the pub's signature chateaubriand of Wiltshire beef for two, as well as a five-course tasting menu.

Trencherman's tip: visitors can turn their trip into an enticing gourmet retreat by booking a room at Troutbeck, the pub's five-bedroom boutique guesthouse overlooking the River Avon. It's worth it for the breakfast alone: a luxe affair of own-smoked ham or salmon served alongside homemade muffins and hollandaise.

Chef Connor Barber-Starkey | **3 course dinner from** £53
Seats 50 | **Bedrooms** 5 | **Room rate from** £170

11 The Castle Inn

Smart pub dining in Castle Combe

West Street, Castle Combe, Chippenham, Wiltshire, SN14 7HN **01249 783030**
thecastleinn.co.uk

At the heart of the Cotswold-stone village of Castle Combe sits this characterful 12th-century coaching house. It's a well-loved spot where those who've spent the day rambling the countryside or teeing off at sister venue The Manor House's 18-hole golf course gather to feast on authentic country fare.

Satiation can be found in head chef Jamie Barnett's crowd-pleasing two AA rosette menus which offer an upmarket take on traditional pub classics. In summer, ravenous patrons devour the likes of wild boar lasagne with Tunworth cheese, summer truffle and herb salad while sitting out on the sunny terrace. In winter, a cosy dining room with log fire awaits. For special celebrations and group dinners, the Oak Room offers intimate private dining for up to 12.

It's a known truth that a hearty supper often leads to a sleepy head, so make a night of it by booking one of the The Castle Inn's sumptuously furnished rooms. With their charming period features and calming colour palette, sound slumber is assured.

Trencherman's tip: guests can also enjoy a fine dining experience by booking the tasting menu in Michelin-starred restaurant Bybrook at The Manor House.

Chef Jamie Barnett | **3 course dinner from** £30
Seats 40 | **Bedrooms** 12 | **Room rate from** £155

12 Sign of the Angel

Historic and romantic inn

6 Church Street, Lacock, Chippenham, Wiltshire, SN15 2LB **01249 730230**
signoftheangel.co.uk

If you're looking for a dining experience with oodles of history and a romantic atmosphere, Sign of the Angel offers it in spades.

Creaking wonky floorboards, stone fireplaces and winding stairways make this inn a favourable dining destination for fans of period dramas and historical romances.

The stone cottages and cobbled streets of the National Trust-owned village of Lacock have appeared in many a costume drama, including *Pride and Prejudice* and *Downton Abbey*.

Whether you're visiting for a light lunch or a special evening meal, the dining ethos at this pub is purposely relaxed and easygoing. On a summer's day there's also a beautiful garden where you can enjoy small plates, salads and cream teas next to a babbling stream.

In winter, the oak-panelled lounge, with its antique furniture and stone floors, is a characterful spot in which to linger over an aperitif before heading into a candlelit dining area of intimate nooks and open fires.

The 15th-century coaching inn may retain much of its original charm but the dining offering showcases the best of modern British cooking.

Chef Ashley Jackson makes it his mission to seek out sustainable produce from farmers, growers and butchers in order to craft classics like duo of lamb (cutlets and stuffed breast), pork tenderloin, and fish dishes paired with prime Cotswold fruit and veg. There's a very tempting offer of three courses for £29 at lunch, with plenty of options for vegetarian and vegan diners.

Homely rooms with original features offer the opportunity for -full exploration of a drinks list that includes local damson vodka and Lacock Gin.

Chef Ashley Jackson | **3 course dinner from** £35
Seats 50 | **Bedrooms** 5 | **Room rate from** £110

Somerset, Bristol & Bath

**Restaurants listed in the guide
correspond to the numbers plotted
on the map.**

All locations are approximate

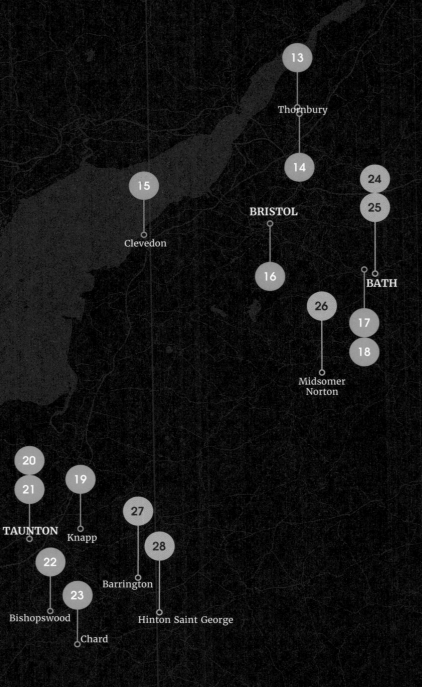

13

Thornbury

14

24

25

15

BRISTOL

Clevedon

16

BATH

26

17

18

Midsomer
Norton

20

21

19

TAUNTON   Knapp

27

22

28

23

Barrington

Bishopswood

Hinton Saint George

Chard

13 Thornbury Castle

Splendid fare at Henry's Tudor pile

Castle Street, Thornbury, Bristol, BS35 1HH **01454 281182**
thornburycastle.co.uk

History buffs and fine-dining enthusiasts alike will be enamoured by this unique staycation destination near Bristol. Once the property of Henry VIII, Thornbury Castle is now a luxury Relais & Châteaux hotel which blends its Tudor splendour with the best of 21st-century hospitality.

England's most notorious ruler may have only spent ten days at his grand pile on the south Gloucestershire border, yet the interiors of this striking castle are dressed as if it's expecting a second visit at any moment.

On the oak-panelled walls of the historic dining rooms hang gold-framed portraits of his relatives, while the guestrooms are furnished with the kind of palatial four-poster beds and opulent fabrics you'd expect of royal quarters.

Executive chef Carl Cleghorn's refined dishes perfectly complement this grand setting. Using the finest locally sourced and castle-grown produce, he crafts classic European dishes executed to the highest standards.

Whether you plump for the à la carte or tasting menu, dinner starts with drinks beside a roaring fire in the lavish drawing room and your evening is punctuated with little surprises such as canapés and amuse bouche.

A fantastic wine list makes it a cinch to find the perfect pairing for dishes such as Loch Duart salmon ravioli with crevette and shellfish bisque. The friendly front of house team know the menu well and are on hand with recommendations to help diners navigate the many pages of old- and new-world wines.

Chef Carl Cleghorn | **6 course tasting menu** £92
Seats 50 | **Bedrooms** 26 | **Room rate from** £249

14 Ronnie's of Thornbury

Modern British cooking in an intimate setting

11 St Mary Street, Thornbury, Bristol, BS35 2AB **01454 411137**
ronnies-restaurant.co.uk

In 2007, Ron Faulkner established Ronnie's in this 17th-century building and it has since become a reliable gourmet go-to for Thornbury's discerning diners.

Chef patron Ron, who was a finalist in the Best Chef category of the Food Reader Awards 2022, runs a tight ship to deliver beautifully prepared seasonal dishes at his cosily intimate restaurant.

The experience may be crafted by a tiny team, but everything is made from scratch on-site using local ingredients of provenance. The result is a delightful culinary adventure.

A tasting menu with matched wine flight provides the zenith of Ron's gourmet offering and comprises six courses such as confit rabbit and ham hock pressé with pickled cauliflower, soused carrot, silver skinned onion and prune.

A short but sweet à la carte menu for lunch and dinner delivers the likes of curried monkfish, lentil dal, Granny Smith apple and coconut foam, while the grazing menu is perfect for an informal lunch. The opportunity to feast on keenly priced small plates of Wye Valley asparagus tart with fermented black garlic and Godminster custard, and salmon pastrami with dill pickled cucumber make it an everyday gourmet treat.

Trencherman's tip: Sunday lunch at Ronnie's goes way beyond the usual fare. Starters such as crispy crab cannelloni with charred pineapple and pepper gel, and mains like 32-day-aged roast sirloin with yorkshire pudding and watercress salad (plus all the trimmings) will surprise and delight.

Chef Ron Faulkner | **3 course dinner from** £55 | **Seats** 36

15 Puro

Flavour-forward dining in Clevedon

Rear of 32–34 Hill Road, Clevedon, Somerset, BS21 7PH **01275 217373**

purorestaurant.co.uk

Since it opened in 2017, Puro has built a reputation as a restaurant that delivers bold flavours, flawless presentation and slick service.

So when, at the end of 2021, new head chef Hayden Botha stepped up to the pass, Puro's loyal patrons collectively held their breath as they waited to discover if he would take their beloved neighbourhood restaurant in a new direction.

Thankfully for them, and for the many visitors who make the pilgrimage to Clevedon to dine at Puro, he hasn't attempted to reinvent the wheel – just given it his own spin.

Big flavours still reign supreme on the generous evening menus, which makes sense

when you know that Hayden previously worked with former head chef Nick Fenlon at The Pump House in Bristol.

Crowd-pleasing dishes such as whole Cornish sole with brown butter shrimps, new potatoes and braised fennel are complemented by a comprehensive wine list and expert recommendations from Puro's owner Dom Lamy.

Make time to pay a visit to sister bottle shop and bar, Vintage & Vine (upstairs), before settling in for an indulgent dinner in the sleek below-ground dining room.

Chef Hayden Botha | **Tasting menu** £55 | **Seats** 40, plus 8 outside

16 Harvey Nichols Second Floor Restaurant

Gilded and glamorous in Bristol

27 Philadelphia Street, Quakers Friars, Bristol, BS1 3BZ **01179 168899**
harveynichols.com/restaurant/bristol-dining

The gold-slicked Second Floor Restaurant inside Bristol's luxury department store isn't necessarily the first place you'd look for seasonal and local cooking, but the team revel in surpassing diners' expectations.

Harvey Nichols' in-house restaurant has built a gleaming reputation for delivering smart, crowd-pleasing menus crafted with creative flair. Just like the ever-changing collections in the clothing department, dishes shift with the seasons and in line with what's fresh, ripe and available from the South West's bountiful larder.

Treat yourself to a well-deserved lunch break in the middle of a shopping trip around Bristol – it'll feed your soul as well as your exhausted body – and take advantage of the Market Menus, which are priced extremely keenly and updated each month. Or make a date for dinner with friends (this is definitely supper-with-the-gang territory) and settle in for a sociable evening at this oasis in the city.

Even afternoon tea is given the five-star treatment: expect the likes of cucumber, mascarpone and poppy-seed sandwiches and homemade patisserie, served with a flute of Champagne.

Trencherman's tip: kick off dinner in style with an aperitif at the NYC-chic bar next door, which ups the glam factor further via moody lighting and a list of well-crafted drinks.

Chef Lucy Lourenco | **3 course dinner from** £30 | **Seats** 60

HALLGARTEN
& NOVUM WINES

Wine supplier to the UK's finest hospitality venues
International Wine Challenge On-Trade Supporter of the Year 2021

17 **The Bath Priory**

Gastronomic getaway in the city

Weston Road, Bath, BA1 2XT **01225 331922**
thebathpriory.co.uk

This elegant boutique hotel is just a short stroll from Bath's buzzy centre but, because it's surrounded by four acres of award-winning gardens, it feels a world away.

Tasteful furnishings, art and architecture create a quintessentially English setting for head chef Jauca Catalin's French-inspired menus. Fresh local produce is used in exciting dishes which showcase exceptional flavours and balance.

Feast on creations presented with artful finesse such as Cornish wild turbot with scallop mousse, carrot and ginger puree and lemongrass sauce. Note, the bread is fabulous but desserts such as apricot soufflé with toffee ice cream and sauce are worth saving room for.

An exemplary wine cellar and experienced sommelier are on hand to provide judicious pairings for every course.

This fine-dining experience is found in the three AA rosette restaurant which has views over the gardens. However, there's also a more casual option in the form of The Pantry & Terrace which offers lighter dishes for breakfast, brunch, lunch and supper.

Trencherman's tip: in good weather, The Pantry & Terrace is an amazing spot for alfresco dining and drinking, especially in early summer when the wisteria that stretches over the golden Cotswold stone is in full bloom.

Chef Jauca Catalin | **3 course dinner from** £70
Seats 27 | **Bedrooms** 33 | **Room rate from** £280

18 The Olive Tree Restaurant

Michelin-starred glamour in Bath

4-7 Russell Street, Bath, BA1 2QF **01225 447928**
olivetreebath.co.uk

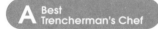
A Best Trencherman's Chef

Gourmet gadabouts looking to spend a foodie weekend in Bath should book a room at The Queensberry Hotel and dine in its basement restaurant, The Olive Tree.

Located on a quiet street, a stone's throw from the historic city's famous attractions, the boutique hotel appeals both to visitors who want to take in the sights and those who'd rather unwind with a book in the courtyard garden. Beautifully styled bedrooms lavished with luxe mod cons make the idea of staying put even more tempting.

However guests choose to spend their day, dinner at The Olive Tree is a guaranteed highlight. Trencherman's Award-winning executive head chef Chris Cleghorn earned a Michelin star for the restaurant in 2018 and has retained it ever since.

Contemporary six- and nine-course tasting menus are the order of the day at The Olive Tree, taking diners on a culinary tour of Chris' talents.

Dishes are complex and multifaceted but centre on a seasonal hero ingredient which showcases the best of British produce. Wiltshire lamb rump, for example, is accompanied by lettuce, anchovy, ewe's curd and mint. There are also vegetarian, vegan and dairy-free editions of the tasting menus.

The exceptional dining experience is complemented by a knowledgeable and friendly front-of-house team and a notable wine list.

Trencherman's tip: make time for a top-drawer cocktail in the intimate Q Bar before dinner.

Chef Chris Cleghorn | **6 course dinner from** £105
Seats 42 | **Bedrooms** 29 | **Room rate from** £135

19 The Rising Sun Knapp

Quality cooking in the countryside

Knapp Road, Knapp, Taunton, Somerset, TA3 6BG **01823 491027**
therisingsunknapp.co.uk

This new addition to the Somerset dining scene is one to visit before word gets out, as it's a notable find for anyone looking for quality cooking in the countryside.

Chef Olly Jackson and front of house Rebecca Jackson are certainly not newbies to the county: they ran the five-star Langford Fivehead Hotel for many years before it was sold. Happily, this dovetailed with the availability of The Rising Sun in the tiny village of Knapp, so the couple seized the opportunity to do something fresh.

In this new venture, they've taken their experience of smart service and crafting beautiful food and woven it into the more casual confines of a charming country pub.

Quality cooking is the hook on which the experience hangs, which is clear from the walls of classic cookbooks that line the rooms of the ancient pub. Escoffier's *A Guide to Modern Cooking* and *River Cottage Handbooks* cram the shelves while dishes such as pan-fried turbot fillet with broccoli, pea puree, parmentier potatoes and tartare butter sauce adorn the tables.

Puds and homemade bread are as top-notch as the savoury dishes and crafted with an attention to detail highly unusual in such laid-back surrounds.

Friendly and unfussy service, a joyful wine list (with plenty of picks by the glass), a pub garden for summer feasting and a huge fireplace for winter cosiness tick all the pub-dining boxes.

Trencherman's tip: the pub's Sunday lunch (not served in school summer holidays) is definitely worth a winding drive through narrow country lanes.

Chef Olly Jackson | **3 course dinner from** £35 | **Seats** 35

20 Augustus

Neighbourhood bistro with class

3 The Courtyard, St James Street, Taunton, Somerset, TA1 1JR **01823 324354**
augustustaunton.co.uk

Taunton's favourite bistro has been burnishing a solid reputation since Cedric Chirossel and Richard Guest decided to set up their own restaurant 11 years ago.

Hospitality is at the heart of the operation and Cedric takes pride in looking after the legion of loyal customers who visit for informal but beautifully cooked lunches and suppers.

Richard's menus are built around high-quality locally sourced ingredients, most of which are delivered or collected on foot from local independents, including greengrocer Granny Smiths, fishmonger Phil Bowditch and nearby Riverside Butchers.

There's French influence in Richard's cooking which he translates into crowd-pleasing dishes such as sirloin steak with tarragon butter, hash brown, watercress and shallot salad, and slow-roasted duck with potatoes anna, creamed greens and duck jus.

The simplicity of good ingredients cooked with skill, a well-considered wine list and on-point service in an unpretentious town centre setting is somewhat rare, making this a special spot.

Trencherman's tip: Augustus recently received a delightful review from Jay Rayner in *The Guardian*, so expect competition for tables to be stiff for a while – book well ahead.

Chef Richard Guest | **3 course dinner from** £35 | **Seats** 40

21 The Castle at Taunton

Comfortable glamour in the heart of town

Castle Green, Taunton, Somerset, TA1 1NF **01823 272671**
the-castle-hotel.com

This smart hotel has retained its reputation as a stalwart of style in Taunton for decades. During that time it's been home to numerous talented chefs and is currently under the stewardship of head chef Andrew Swann.

You don't need to be a resident at the hotel to enjoy its various gourmet offerings, which include the elegant Art-Deco-style Castle Bow restaurant. Its stained-glass windows provide a smart setting for afternoon tea.

Private dining options are plentiful and include the luxurious Penthouse with panoramic views of Taunton and the Quantocks, which is available for 6-16 guests.

The more casual Brazz is a buzzy restaurant kitted out in contemporary decor. It's a favourite in the county town for laid-back lunching, drinks and casual suppers. To get the full vibe, order the house special of Brazz fish cakes which have been on the menu since the restaurant opened in 1998.

High-quality South West ingredients form the backbone of The Castle's menus and include the likes of Quantock lamb and Brixham crab. In the summer, guests can dine alfresco in the 12th-century walled gardens.

Trencherman's tip: if you can, stay the night. The attractive bedrooms are supremely comfortable, and the hotel is situated right in the centre of town for easy exploration on foot.

Chef Andrew Swann | **3 course dinner from** £30
Seats 70 | **Bedrooms** 44 | **Room rate from** £120

22 Candlelight Inn

Fresh setting for rural pub dining

Bishopswood, Chard, Somerset, TA20 3RS **01460 234476**
candlight-inn.co.uk

The concept of candlelit dinners feels a bit old-school – conjouring images of formal dining a deux – so be prepared to have your preconceptions snuffed out at Candlelight Inn.

Owners Mike and Simon Rose-Macleod have given the charming 17th-century pub a tasteful and contemporary makeover via country-living styling and smart food, and the result is fabulous.

You have to put in the effort to get there – it's uber rural, in the heart of the Blackdown Hills – but every country mile is worth it for chef Aaron Ashworth's cooking and the friendly service from Mike and team.

Go casual and order from the pub menu in the very attractive bar. Or book a table in the beams-and-fireplace dining area where a more upscale menu is complemented by hedgerow flowers on the table and, of course, flickering candles.

Beautifully prepared multidimensional dishes showcase local produce (including ingredients from the garden) and in appropriate portion sizes, so you can still do pudding with aplomb.

Trencherman's tip: swing by early so there's time for an aperitif G&T made with the pub's own artisan gin, Beau (named after Mike and Simon's irish setter).

Chef Aaron Ashworth | **3 course dinner from** £40 | **Seats** 85

23 The Cotley Inn

Field-to-fork dining in the Blackdown Hills

Wambrook, Chard, Somerset, TA20 3EN **01460 62348**
cotleyinnwambrook.co.uk

Spend an evening on The Cotley Inn's lavender-fringed terrace and you'll get the pleasure of dining on delicious seasonal fare while also drinking in the views of the fields in which it was grown and reared.

The contemporary country inn is a Grade II-listed former farmhouse and sits in the heart of the Cotley Estate in the Blackdown Hills. Being part of the estate provides head chef Dan Brown with an abundance of ultra-fresh produce, including veg from the kitchen garden, Ruby Red beef, rare-breed pork and chicken.

With the help of sous chef Danny Baker, Dan puts this bounty to fantastic use in modern interpretations of classic pub dishes such as

the Cotley Estate Ruby Red beef burger, and a chorizo and Cotley Blue mac 'n' cheese. Those looking for something a touch more refined will find it on the à la carte line-up which includes the likes of seaweed-crusted brill with pea and house-pancetta fricassee, and Cotley Estate venison haunch with confit tomatoes, venison ragu and rosemary polenta.

Since taking over the dining pub in 2018, Ben Porter and Maddie Beaumont have been steadily renovating the building – the latest addition being a quartet of country-chic bedrooms. Book one so you can fully explore the wine list and wake up to the sound of birdsong and the cows in the field next door.

Chefs Dan Brown and Danny Baker | **3 course dinner from** £35
Seats 60 | **Bedrooms** 4 | **Room rate from** £125

24 The Beckford Bottle Shop

Bistro chic in Bath

5-8 Saville Row, Bath, BA1 2QP **01225 809302**
beckfordbottleshop.com

The Beckford Bottle Shop has been popular with Bath locals and in-the-know visitors since it was established in 2015. However, the buzz around the bistro and wine merchant went stratospheric in 2022 following two events: a glowing review by *The Guardian* critic Jay Rayner and winning Best Restaurant in the Food Reader Awards.

Part of The Beckford Group (a small collection of quality pubs and restaurants in Somerset and Wiltshire), Beckford Bottle Shop specialises in doing simple things well. In the restaurant, a superb collection of wines from the adjoining bottle shop complements artisan cheeses, charcuterie boards and small plates crafted from seasonal and local produce.

Head chef James Harris doesn't overcomplicate dishes, opting for flavour over frills. Expect ingredient-led small plates which put West Country produce front and centre – think Bath chaps with Bramley apple, and cured ChalkStream trout with fennel and wild garlic flowers.

The effortlessly cool setting makes the perfect backdrop for all manner of occasions – from impromptu lunches to milestone celebrations. In summer, graze on local charcuterie and wines by the glass under the alfresco awning. On colder days, retreat to the basement dining room where low lighting, dark wood and original features make for an alluring dinner destination.

Chef James Harris | **3 course dinner from** £25 | **Seats** 60

25 Robun

Fusion thrills and creative cocktails

4 Princes Buildings, George Street, Bath, BA1 2ED **01225 614424**
robun.co.uk

It's hard to find great Japanese food that goes beyond sushi and tempura in London, let alone the South West, so to find a restaurant doing a modern take on yakiniku (the art of grilling meat, seafood and vegetables over a traditional robata charcoal fire) in the centre of Bath is quite something.

Robun opened on George Street in July 2021 and quickly made a name for itself as one of the city's most exciting dining spots. Jon Claro worked at some of the capital's best pan-Asian restaurants (The Ivy Asia, Sticks'n'Sushi and Pen Yen at Soho Farmhouse) before stepping into the role of head chef at Robun, where he leads a talented brigade.

Visit to try hero dishes such as pan-fried sea bream with truffled ponzu sauce, iberico baby pork ribs with soy and mirin, and grass-fed beef filled with Japanese pickles. If you're of an indecisive nature, take the sharing route and sample small plates that include panko soft-shell crab with nuoc cham sauce, wagyu sliders in brioche buns, and katsuobushi takoyaki (traditional octopus dumplings with bonito flakes).

Sake fans will be thrilled to find a comprehensive list available by both glass and bottle. There's also a fantastic line-up of creative cocktails and Japanese whiskies.

Chef Jon Claro | **3 course dinner from** £29 | **Seats** 76

TRENCHERMAN'S

Guide
30

NOBLE ISLE

A fine fragrance, bath and body brand inspired by the rich
cultural heritage of the British Isles

nobleisle.com

No-compromise sustainable dining

Stratton Road, Holcombe, Somerset, BA3 5EB **01761 232478**
theholcombe.com

When chefs Alan Lucas and Caroline Gardiner relocated from London to rural Somerset they were keen for their new project to be as sustainable as possible. In taking over The Holcombe near Radstock they've realised that ambition and created one of the greenest restaurants with rooms in the county.

The 17th-century inn is surrounded by two acres of land on which Alan and Caroline, with gardener Kirsty, grow fruits, vegetables, herbs and flowers for The Holcombe's hyper-seasonal menus. What can't be cultivated on-site is sourced from local Somerset producers. The same ethos extends to the meat and fish.

Any kitchen food waste is composted, while cooking oil is recycled into biodiesel. The duo have also rewilded areas of their land to benefit wildlife and introduced a beehive to harvest Holcombe honey.

Head chef Alan's menus change daily depending on the kitchen-garden harvest. Dishes are creative, beautifully presented and packed with flavour. Expect to encounter the likes of local Castlemead chicken with asparagus, baby gem and white onion velouté.

In summer, the covered Mediterranean-style garden with views over Downside Abbey is the best spot to enjoy Alan's cooking and sample the homemade flavoured gins.

Trencherman's tip: extend your trip by booking one of the gorgeous country-chic guestrooms or dog-friendly lodges.

Chef Alan Lucas | **3 course dinner from** £40
Seats 45 | **Bedrooms** 11 | **Room rate from** £170

27 The Barrington Boar

Crowd-pleasing contemporary pub dining

Main Street, Barrington, Ilminster, Somerset, TA19 0JB **01460 259281**
thebarringtonboar.co.uk

'Refined comfort food' **is how Alasdair Clifford describes his style of cooking at this contemporary country pub near Ilminster. The chef, who previously worked at Chez Bruce and The Glasshouse, returned to his home county in 2018 to take over The Barrington Boar with his wife Victoria Collins.**

The duo refreshed the pub's interior and menu to create a stylish setting in which to feast with friends and family. Working closely with local farmers, foragers and cheesemongers, Alasdair crafts gratifying dishes that offer a taste of the local terroir.

He and Victoria also collaborate with regional breweries and offer an ever-changing collection of ales and ciders. South West spirits such as Wicked Wolf Gin and Somerset Cider Brandy also feature, along with Smith & Evans sparkling wine which is made less than ten miles from Barrington.

The delights extend beyond the food and drinks as there are four contemporary bedrooms on-site, making this a fantastic base from which to explore the east Somerset and Dorset countryside.

Trencherman's tip: Sunday lunch at The Barrington Boar is pretty special. Choose between slow-roast Somerset sirloin, Yarrow Hey Farm pork belly and broad bean and grelot onion vol-au-vent, all of which are served with roasties cooked in dripping, sky-high yorkshires, glazed carrots and cauliflower cheese.

Chef Alasdair Clifford | **3 course dinner from** £36.55
Seats 45 | **Bedrooms** 4 | **Room rate from** £113

28 The Lord Poulett Arms

Effortless countryside glamour

High Street, Hinton Saint George, Somerset, TA17 8SE **01460 73149**

lordpoulettarms.com

When you imagine a gourmet getaway at a stylish rural pub in Somerset, chances are you'll picture something very similar to this gorgeous thatched inn.

Six beautifully designed bedrooms above a honey-coloured pub make the tiny village of Hinton Saint George a very desirable destination for city dwellers seeking peace and luxury. Each guestroom has been thoughtfully designed to complement the pub's 17th-century origins and comes stocked with sumptuous Bramley bath products. Peaceful slumber is guaranteed thanks to Siberian goose-down bedding, and the five-star treatment continues with complimentary Bloody Marys and fizz at breakfast.

Anyone spending the night at The Lord Poulett Arms would be crazy to pass on the opportunity to dine there too, as head chef Philip Verden excels in giving classic British dishes the LPA treatment. Favourites such as pork and bacon faggots with mash, cabbage and onion gravy are crafted from impeccable local ingredients.

A spacious courtyard also makes this a popular lunch spot on sunny days. Order a glass of chilled rosé from the short but well-considered wine list and pair it with something seasonal such as burrata with panzanella salad and truffled dressing.

Chef Philip Verden | **3 course dinner from** £28
Seats 44 | **Bedrooms** 6 | **Room rate from** £95

Dorset & Hampshire

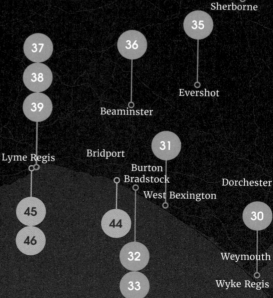

Upton

(40)

Andover

**Restaurants listed in the guide
correspond to the numbers plotted
on the map.**

All locations are approximate

Fontmell Magna

(41)

New Milton

Poole   Christchurch

BOURNEMOUTH

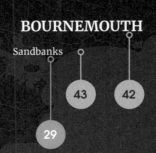

Sandbanks

(43)   (42)

(29)

29 Rick Stein Sandbanks

Smart seafood and stunning views

10-14 Banks Road, Sandbanks, Poole, Dorset, BH13 7QB **01202 283000**
rickstein.com

Spectacular views across Poole Harbour provide a glittering backdrop to an evening of feasting at Rick Stein Sandbanks, the Dorset outpost of the Stein collective.

The main restaurant on the first floor offers The Seafood Restaurant classics like fruits de mer and dover sole à la meunière. For casual daytime dishes, such as moules marinières, the downstairs bar is the go-to. It's also a great spot for a luxurious celebration brunch.

While seafood steals the limelight in both dining areas, committed carnivores and veggies are also extremely well catered for. Just as Rick's fish-focused recipes are inspired by his travels around the world, so are plant-based creations such as vegetable makhanawala curry, and ravioli of caramelised onion and fennel seeds served with sun-dried tomatoes, porcini mushrooms and hazelnuts.

Service is as good as the food: the restaurant scooped the Trencherman's Award for Best Front of House Team in 2020.

Chef Sam Hughes | **3 course dinner from** £34 | **Seats** 145

30 Crab House Cafe

Superb seafood with views to match

Ferryman's Way, Portland Road, Wyke Regis, Dorset, DT4 9YU **01305 788867**
crabhousecafe.co.uk

While most chefs talk in food miles, the team at this coastal restaurant count in metres for much of their seafood-centred menu.

Despite the name, the star attraction at Crab House Cafe is actually its oysters. Grown just a short paddle from the restaurant's tables – at the on-site oyster farm – the prized bivalves are fabulously fresh and plump. Make like a local and slurp them, au naturel, from their shells.

What's not cultivated in-house is sourced as locally as possible. Most of the seafood is landed at nearby Weymouth and Poole, veg comes from local growers, and milk and cheese via The Open Air Dairy in Littlebredy.

Crab House Cafe owner Nigel Bloxham (who sourced fish for the likes of Keith Floyd before opening his own restaurant) favours native fish species, prioritising sustainability over trends.

The daily menu is supplemented by a long list of specials which makes deciding what to order quite a challenge. Classic dishes, such as turbot hollandaise and roasted lemon sole, vie for diners' attention with creative compilations such as baked red mullet with golden beetroot and cauliflower.

Pair your pick with a glass of Dorset wine – the Bride Valley Chardonnay is a marvellous match for almost everything on the menu.

Chef George Brace | **3 course dinner from** £34 | **Seats** 43

31 The Club House

Seaside-smart at West Bexington

1 Beach Road, West Bexington, Dorset, DT2 9DG **01308 898302**

theclubhousewestbexington.co.uk

This Chesil Beach restaurant is set in a 1930s Olympic-pool clubhouse and retains many of the building's original features.

The Club House's interiors are best described as mid-century modern meets New England nautical and provide a fitting backdrop for new head chef Liam Smith's seafood-focused seasonal menus.

Top-notch fresh ingredients from local fishermen and farmers, as well as from the restaurant's own kitchen garden, form the basis of the AA rosette dishes.

An innovative cocktail menu signposts the perfect way to start an evening at The Club House: check out concoctions like Toast of Chesil Beach – toast-infused Black Cow vodka, lime juice, marmalade, honey syrup and toast crumbs.

Then take a seat on the heated outdoor deck and survey the stunning views of the Jurassic Coast as you sip your drink and nibble on crispy tempura oysters.

The menu features local favourites such as West Bay lobster and Chesil smoked salmon, alongside plenty of globally inspired meat and veggie options.

Those looking to host a small party should also check out the private dining area, located in a separate beach house in the garden.

Trencherman's tip: searching for a unique venue for a special occasion? The Club House is licensed and has a helipad, so you can arrive in style.

Chef Liam Smith | **3 course dinner from** £35 | **Seats** 65

Photo: Ed Schofield

32 The Seaside Boarding House

Unparalleled views over Lyme Bay

Cliff Road, Burton Bradstock, Dorset, DT6 4RB **01308 897205**

theseasideboardinghouse.com

Set on the cliffs overlooking Dorset's sweeping Chesil Beach and Lyme Bay, The Seaside Boarding House is a real treasure to be discovered on the Jurassic Coast.

Whether visiting for lunch or dinner, diners can look forward to feasting on modern British dishes which champion seasonal produce from Dorset's fishing boats, farms and smallholdings.

When the weather's good, enjoy the edible delights on the terrace overlooking Chesil Beach. Don't fret if the alfresco tables are full as the restaurant's large patio doors are flung open when the sun's out.

The terrace is also a popular spot for a signature cocktail, a glass of fizz or a nightcap under the stars. When the sea breezes pick up, head indoors to the attractive bar.

Trencherman's tip: if you're looking for somewhere to stay during your coastal adventures, you'll find nine smart bedrooms upstairs with unrivalled sea views.

Chef Seldon Curry | **3 course dinner from** £60
Seats 60 | **Bedrooms** 9 | **Room rate from** £245

33 Three Horseshoes Pub & Kitchen

A Best Newcomer

Asian-inspired seafood thrills

Mill Street, Burton Bradstock, Dorset, DT6 4QZ **01308 897259**

threehorseshoesburtonbradstock.co.uk

Swing by this Trencherman's Award winner for restaurant-quality dishes served in an environment where you don't have to dress to impress to eat well. Not that Three Horseshoes isn't charmingly attractive, it simply lacks pretension.

Talented Dutch chef-patron Jaap Schep runs the kitchen while his wife Hannah manages front of house, the pair delighting diners with an offer steeped in local seafood. A good proportion of the menu is fish focused and influenced by all corners of the globe: seafood bouillabaisse sits next to dressed Portland crab and Indonesian seafood curry.

Pan-Asian flavour profiles are Jaap's go-to, and diners chasing chilli thrills will find them in dishes as diverse as crispy smoked-Chesil-mackerel bao bun with mango, peanut and thai-basil salad, and a storming bang bang cauliflower with firecracker sauce.

The latter is one of an exciting list of bar snacks which, in quantity, could kick plans for a starter, main and pud into touch. Who wouldn't enjoy working their way through small plates of Dutch bitterballen (beef croquettes), Poole Bay oysters, and kibbeling (lightly spiced battered fish bites) paired with wines by the glass?

Chef Jaap Schep | **3 course dinner from** £32 | **Seats** 35

34 The Eastbury Hotel & Spa

Elegant escape in Sherborne

Long Street, Sherborne, Dorset, DT9 3BY **01935 813131**
theeastburyhotel.co.uk

For a charming getaway in Dorset, you'd be hard pushed to top a visit to The Eastbury Hotel with its opportunity to step back into a more glamorous age.

Start your evening with a Dorset Viper Gin in the cocktail bar with its retro pin-up imagery and leopard-print carpet. Then move through to the conservatory-style Seasons Restaurant where, if you time it right, your supper may be accompanied by a pianist tickling the ivories.

However delightful the music, it's got serious competition for diners' attention from the excellent cooking by new head chef Henry Osmond. Everything's crafted with confident elegance using locally grown and reared produce and herbs from the kitchen garden.

Feast from crowd-pleasing seasonal menus that include starters such as asparagus with homemade honey-roast ham, poached eggs and hollandaise sauce, and mains of fresh local fish with purple sprouting broccoli, tagliatelle, brown shrimp and a lemon and white wine cream.

The pleasures extend beyond those of the edible variety: a flower-filled walled garden, contemporary bedrooms and a woodland-style boutique spa provide further reasons to prolong your stay.

Chef Henry Osmond | **3 course dinner from** £30
Seats 45 | **Bedrooms** 26 | **Room rate from** £205

TRENCHERMAN'S

Guide
30

PKF
FRANCIS
CLARK
Shared Ambition

Accounting | Advisory | Audit | Tax

pkf-francisclark.co.uk

35 Acorn Inn

Gourmet escape in Hardy country

28 Fore Street, Evershot, Dorset, DT2 0JW **01935 83228**
acorn-inn.co.uk

This 16th-century coaching inn ticks all the classic rural pub boxes thanks to its log fires, oak panelling, bare beams and original skittle alley. However, fantastic food crafted by a team of skilled chefs and a mention in *Tess of the D'Urbervilles* elevate Acorn Inn to a different level altogether.

The Acorn's delicious food pays homage to the surrounding Dorset coast and countryside. Expect to find seasonal compilations that champion local producers; dishes include the likes of rack of Portland lamb with potato and thyme terrine and wild mushrooms.

A more casual bar menu, which features comforting classics such as honey and mustard baked ham with lacy free-range fried eggs and thick cut chips, continues the seasonal and local theme.

An extensive whisky, rum and gin collection, a suite of comfortable bedrooms and the beautiful Dorset setting make it impossible to resist the temptation to linger longer. Whether you're craving a weekend retreat or a casual dinner with friends, this picturesque bolthole should be on your hit list.

Trencherman's tip: if the ten beautifully decorated bedrooms are booked up, check out Acorn Inn's elegant sister establishment, Summer Lodge, nearby.

Chef Ana Martins | **3 course dinner from** £40
Seats 40 | **Bedrooms** 10 | **Room rate from** £140

36 **Brassica Restaurant**

Design-led dining in Dorset

4 The Square, Beaminster, Dorset, DT8 3AS **01308 538100**

brassicarestaurant.co.uk

After running a series of successful restaurants in London, in 2014 chef Cass Titcombe relocated to Dorset with his partner, designer Louise Chidgey, to establish a business that would blend their skills and passions. The result is this design-led, family-run restaurant which puts provenance front and centre.

Cass' cooking is best described as modern European, and he combines local produce with specialist ingredients and influences from Spain and Italy to create dishes that sing with flavour.

The menu changes daily, depending on what the kitchen team can get their hands on as they endeavour to source all fresh ingredients from within 15 miles of the restaurant. There's also a commitment to only serving organic meat and dairy, alongside the dayboat fish and Dorset-grown veggies.

A new brunch menu extends the opportunities to dine at Brassica and includes the likes of smoked haddock with crispy potatoes, spinach and béarnaise butter, and jamón serrano with fried eggs and pangrattato.

Trencherman's tip: no daytime trip to the restaurant would be complete without popping into Brassica Mercantile next door. The homeware, lifestyle and food and drink store is a treasure trove of delicious things to eat and admire – you can even pick up Cass' Brassica at Home meals to feast on later.

Chef Cass Titcombe | **3 course dinner from** £40 | **Seats** 38

37 Millside

Jurassic Coast treasure

1 Mill Lane, Lyme Regis, Dorset, DT7 3PU **01297 445999**
themillside.co.uk

This contemporary restaurant, which is under new ownership, has swiftly distinguished itself as a treasured seafood restaurant on the Jurassic Coast.

Wife and husband team Georgina and John Baker had a tricky start when they took over Millside in late 2019 as, just a few months in, they found themselves thrown into the chaos of the on-off lockdowns. Yet, despite a disruptive start, they quickly earnt a reputation – and two AA rosettes.

John oversees front of house, while Georgina leads a small team in the kitchen. Her globetrotting career – which includes working for the Queen's cousin, Lady Elizabeth Anson – is reflected in the cooking.

Pleasing menus with a natural leaning towards local seafood include delicious classics such as coquilles st jacques – a Lyme Bay scallop tucked beneath layers of whipped potato, parmesan and Lyme Bay Winery Brut cream.

Carnivores are equally well catered for in relaxed-dining dishes such as the Millside spin on ham, egg and chips: Dorset-apple-syrup glazed ham, fried Dorset quail's egg, homemade Cornish new potato crisps and paprika mayonnaise.

Trencherman's tip: warm day? Complement a table on the Mediterranean-style terrace with a bottle of chilled Provençal rosé and a fruits de mer sharing platter.

Chef Georgina Baker | **3 course dinner from** £37.50 | **Seats** 30

38 Robin Wylde

Taste of the Dorset terroir

63a Silver Street, Lyme Regis, Dorset, DT7 3HR **07308 079427**

robinwylde.com

The offer at Robin Wylde is simple: a multi-course tasting menu which provides a snapshot of each micro-season of Lyme's coast and countryside.

It could be considered a risky strategy, but it's paying off for ambitious chef Harriet Mansell. Her polished credentials include having worked with Mark Hix, interned at Noma in Denmark and represented the South West on *Great British Menu* (while Robin Wylde was still just a pop-up). She also picked up Best Chef in the Food Reader Awards 2022.

In October 2020, the restaurant became a permanent fixture with the opening of this bricks-and-mortar site. With just 18 covers it offers a pleasingly intimate dining experience where each course is described to the diner as it's delivered. This is helpful as Harriet

and team scour the surrounding landscape for foraged ingredients, resulting in some delicious but unfamiliar items making their way onto the menu.

Each beautifully presented dish is paired with a glass of something good, usually biodynamic or organic. There's also a very good non-alcoholic drinks flight available, which includes creative homemade brews such as pineapple weed and mint kombucha.

Trencherman's tip: get a second bite of the cherry at Lilac, Robin Wylde's sister venue across town, which specialises in small plates and natural wines.

Chef Harriet Mansell | **Tasting menu from** £85 | **Seats** 18

39 Alexandra Hotel and Restaurant

Luscious luxury in Lyme Regis

Pound Street, Lyme Regis, Dorset, DT7 3HZ **01297 442010**

hotelalexandra.co.uk

Alexandra Hotel and Restaurant sits high on the hill above Lyme Regis. The setting is so lush and escapist that, in summer, diners find themselves inexorably drawn to a postprandial stroll through the gardens to take in the astonishing seascape below.

It's a lovely spot to wander – glass of fizz in hand – and enjoy a moment of tranquillity, especially after a day in the bustling town or fossil hunting on the beach.

The views and mature gardens are complemented by smart interiors designed in eclectic country-style. There's something interesting to catch the eye on every shelf and wall – especially in the maritime-themed sitting room. However, beyond all these attractions, foodies favour the 18th-century hotel for its contemporary British cooking.

Choose between two restaurant experiences: the Ammonite restaurant in the orangery is a vision of floral loveliness, thanks to its elegant decor and views over the attractive gardens (it's also got a glassed-over ancient well in the middle of the floor). Or pick the cool blues of the seashell-adorned Alexandra Restaurant for evening feasting – it's especially lovely by the glow of candlelight.

Trencherman's tip: for special romantic occasions, private dining for two in the Lookout Tower is a delightful option – and if your significant other says 'yes' you could even return to get hitched in the hotel's old chapel.

Chef Chris Chatfield | **3 course dinner from** £30
Seats 70 | **Bedrooms** 23 | **Room rate from** £180

40 The Crown Inn

French cooking meets modern rustic

Village Street, Upton, Andover, Hampshire, SP11 0JS **01264 736044**
crownupton.co.uk

It's difficult to beat a long sociable supper with friends at a classic country dining pub, and The Crown Inn at Upton is just the kind of place you'd want to do it.

The cottage-style village inn has been gently modernised to create a relaxed restaurant environment that's a fitting backdrop to Dave Watts' clever cooking. The chef patron's efforts paid off in 2021 when The Crown Inn was awarded a Michelin plate.

Dave, who trained under Raymond Blanc, specialises in contemporary French dishes which focus on provenance. Most of the ingredients on his menus (choose between the classic pub line-up, plats du jour menu or à la carte offering) are sourced from small-scale, artisan producers.

This is a place to gather with friends, order a couple of bottles of wine and tuck into memorable dishes such as confit hake with herbed quinoa, romesco, toasted almonds and croutons.

In summer, the beer garden is usually abuzz with sociable chatter and alfresco feasting, while the menu showcases fresh seasonal dishes such as open lasagne of violet artichokes, purple sprouting broccoli and asparagus with herb emulsion.

Chef Dave Watts | **3 course dinner from** £18.50 | **Seats** 65

41 The Fontmell

Contemporary dining inn

Crown Hill, Fontmell Magna, Shaftesbury, Dorset, SP7 0PA **01747 811441**

thefontmell.co.uk

Sourcing the best produce money can buy is priority number one for the team at this modern Dorset inn.

Pork, for example, is sourced from a family farm a stone's throw from The Fontmell. Owner John Crompton ensures the whole animal is put to delicious use in pub classics like the Sunday roast (where it's served with all the incredible trimmings), rustic homemade sausage rolls at the bar, and as thick-cut bacon and own-recipe sausages in the generous full English breakfasts.

The charming village inn is naturally split into two dining areas by a babbling brook which flows between the cosy bar and smarter restaurant – though both sides offer an attractive setting for high quality modern British cooking.

If the weather's good, there's also an alfresco dining area in the garden where the team turn out artisan pizzas from the wood-fired oven.

Whether you're indulging in three courses from the fine-dining menu, tucking into rustic fish and chips by the fire or sharing a family-style supper outside, the vibe is relaxed and friendly.

The delectable drinks line-up includes an exceptional handpicked wine list and The Fontmell's own house beer, Sibeth Ale (brewed at nearby Keystone Brewery).

With the option to stay the night in one of the six modern country bedrooms, it's a great venue for a weekend getaway.

3 course dinner from £25 | **Seats** 46 | **Bedrooms** 6 | **Room rate from** £80

42 Captain's Club Hotel & Spa

Modern riverside dining

Wick Ferry, Christchurch, Dorset, BH23 1HU **01202 475111**

captainsclubhotel.com

In summer, Christchurch is abuzz with staycationers seeking sun, seafood and Champagne – and those in the know head to Captain's Club Hotel.

The modern four-star hotel is located on the banks of the River Stour (a swift five-minute walk from the historic market town) with many of its chic bedrooms enjoying views over the water and of boats motoring out to sea. It's ideally positioned for a relaxing retreat, which includes sessions in the hotel's spa, hydrotherapy pool and treatment rooms. Dog owners can even take their pooches and benefit from coastal walks.

Richard Allsopp recently took over as head chef, bringing with him a wealth of experience from some of the region's top hotel kitchens. Ocean-fresh fish dishes are the stars of the contemporary menu, although meaty creations such as venison carpaccio and osso buco also deserve their place on deck.

The Club Restaurant offers laid-back indulgence, but in warmer months it pays to secure a seat outside on the sunny terrace for alfresco dining. When the sun sets, slip into the sleek Quay Bar for a digestif.

Chef Richard Allsopp | **3 course dinner from** £35
Seats 120 | **Bedrooms** 29 | **Room rate from** £325

43 WestBeach Restaurant

Alfresco seafood spoils

Pier Approach, Bournemouth, Dorset, BH2 5AA **01202 587785**
west-beach.co.uk

**From its smart deck overlooking
Bournemouth Beach, family-owned
WestBeach Restaurant guarantees dining
with a sea view.**

Amazing seascapes are not the sole attraction,
however, as its design-led open kitchen
gives diners the chance to watch the team of
innovative chefs craft flavourful creations
from top-notch ingredients.

Fresh fish and seafood are the stars of the
show, and the fishermen's catch from local
waters around Bournemouth and Poole form
the lion's share of the enticing menu.

Choose from crowd-pleasers such as plump
mussels cooked in tom yum spices, lobster
with chilli and lime butter, and fantastically
fresh fruits de mer. And, of course, there's no
shame in embracing the classic British fave
of golden beer-battered fish and chips with
mushy peas and tartar sauce.

An exciting and extensive wine list, with
bottles sourced from all over the world, makes
it easy to pair your pick of the menu with a
perfect match.

Trencherman's tip: early risers should stop
by for cracking breakfasts such as WestBeach
crab benedict, avocado on toasted sourdough
and the hearty full English.

Chef Andras Veres | **3 course dinner from** £50 | **Seats** 100

SALCOMBE
GIN®

Exceptional award-winning gin, distilled and crafted in Devon

44 The Station Kitchen

All aboard for fine dining in Bridport

Station Road, West Bay, Bridport, Dorset, DT6 4EW **01308 422845**

thestationkitchen.co.uk

It's always fun to find somewhere a little out of the ordinary for dinner, and a reclaimed first-world-war railway carriage at the seaside certainly fits the bill.

Start your evening with a quality cocktail in the Waiting Room bar before being escorted onto the train where an evening of edible entertainments is about to depart. Not that the train ever actually leaves the station, but stepping aboard and being immersed in The Station Kitchen's fabulously eclectic dining room is rather like taking a trip somewhere fun and free spirited.

The two AA rosette restaurant is a fave with celebs such as Martin Clunes, Hugh Laurie and Olivia Colman who have all booked a ticket to feast on its seasonal dishes crafted from local and organic produce. Many of the ingredients are grown in the Station's kitchen garden.

The cooking is as Instagrammable as the setting and house specialities such as barbecued lobster tail with glazed veal sweetbread, jersey royals, summer salad, sorrel and gooseberry sauce will surprise and delight. A tasting menu – and vegan equivalent – offers a first-class option for special occasions (there's also a private dining room that seats up to six).

Keep an eye on social for new venture The Ticket Office, which is soon to open on the platform and will serve wood-fired pizzas, vibrant salads and heavenly cheesecakes.

Trencherman's tip: book a table before 6pm to take advantage of the kids' Little Loco menu.

Chef Chris Chatfield | **3 course dinner from** £50 | **Seats** 80

45 Tom's Lyme Regis

Seafood with stunning views

Marine Parade, Lyme Regis, Dorset, DT7 3JQ **01297 816018**
tomslymeregis.com

With its historic cobb (made famous by Meryl Streep in *The French Lieutenant's Woman*), Lyme Regis is one of the region's prettiest holiday resorts and this new Marine Parade restaurant makes the most of the town's buzzing beachside vibe.

Tom's Lyme Regis, a pebble's skim from the shoreline, is where chef Tom Robinson prepares all things that come with shells and scales. His daily-changing menu puts the emphasis on the best local fish and produce, which is crafted into simple dishes with imaginative twists.

If you choose to sit out on the terrace, you'll feel cosy and sheltered with the offer of blankets, heaters and parasols, while many of the indoor seats offer stunning views over balmy blue waters. Pause with a glass of fizz from nearby Castlewood Vineyard and take in an ever-changing vista of big skies and lapping waves.

Starters such as Lyme Bay crab croquetas with romesco and gremolata pique the appetite for mains which include pan-roasted cod and sirloin of Dartmoor beef.

Piscine pleasures don't come much better than Tom's Fish Board which heaves under the weight of Dorset lobster, Porthilly rock oysters, Lyme Bay scallops, crab croquetas and kimchi-cured salmon. There's easily enough to feed four and the accompanying saffron aioli, pickles, anchovy butter, chips and mixed leaves add layers of delectable flavour.

For the full experience at this family-run restaurant, don't skip pudding: the likes of chocolate mousse and cherry clafoutis offer modern interpretations of kitchen classics.

Chef Tom Robinson | **3 course dinner from** £37 | **Seats** 28

46 The Oyster & Fish House

Hix fix of fresh fish feasting

Cobb Road, Lyme Regis, Dorset, DT7 3JP **01297 446910**
theoysterandfishhouse.co.uk

Fans of Mark Hix's superb pared-back cooking were thrilled when the chef returned to his Lyme Regis restaurant in July 2020 to reopen HIX as The Oyster & Fish House.

At the solo venture, Mark and head chef Jeremy Bird serve fresh, responsibly sourced fish – simply grilled and on the bone – caught off the Dorset coast. The catch is often from Lyme Bay itself and there's a lovely synergy to tucking into the spoils of the sea while gazing over the coast through floor-to-ceiling windows. The newly built deck skirting the gleaming glass restaurant is *the* place to enjoy a sundowner in Lyme.

Supporting the Lyme Bay Fisheries and Conservation Reserve is one of Mark's top priorities, so the restaurant also cooks bycatch. Beautifully fresh seafood is matched with carefully chosen seasonal ingredients

sourced from local producers. Dishes such as Korean fried monkfish cheeks, shellfish soup with Somerset Cider Brandy, and grilled catch of the day with sea vegetables put the ingredients centre stage without pomp or pretension.

Take a tour of the South West's vineyards via a wine menu in which Lyme Bay Winery and boutique vineyard Castlewood headline the local offering. Alternatives include Dorset-brewed craft beers and seasonal cocktails showcasing local spirits such as Black Cow Pure Milk Vodka.

Encased in glass and with stunning views over The Cobb and out to sea, The Oyster & Fish House is a stunning setting for all manner of occasions – from birthday parties to intimate foodie weddings.

Chef Jeremy Bird | **3 course dinner from** £30 | **Seats** 40

Devon

Restaurants listed in the guide correspond to the numbers plotted on the map.

All locations are approximate

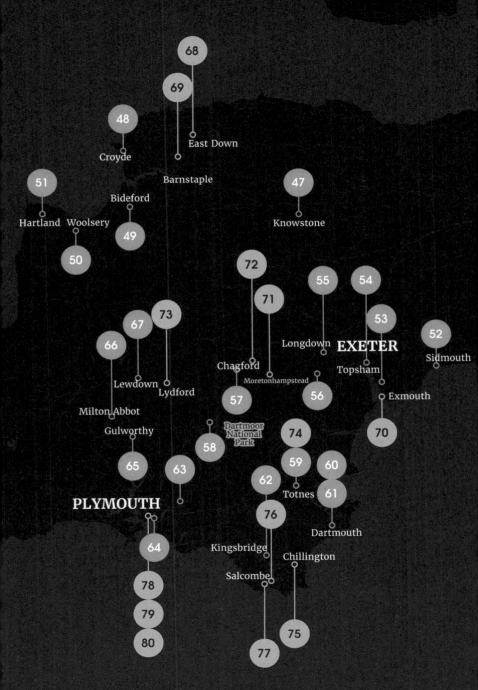

68

69

East Down

48

Croyde

Barnstaple

51

47

Bideford

Hartland   Woolsery

Knowstone

49

50

72

55   54

71

53

EXETER

67   73

Longdown

52

66

Chagford

Topsham

Sidmouth

Lewdown

Moretonhampstead

Lydford

56

Exmouth

Milton Abbot

57

74

70

Gulworthy

Dartmoor
National
Park

58

59

60

65   63

62   Totnes   61

PLYMOUTH

76

Dartmouth

64

Kingsbridge   Chillington

78

Salcombe

79

75

80

77

47 The Masons Arms

Michelin-starred dining on the edge of Exmoor

A Award for Special Contribution

Knowstone, South Molton, Devon, EX36 4RY **01398 341231**
masonsarmsdevon.co.uk

The Masons Arms is a beautiful thatched 13th-century country pub that serves cosy pints by the fire while also being home to a tour de force of fine dining.

For 17 years, Mark and Sarah Dodson have run their Michelin-starred restaurant (they were awarded the star within six months of opening and have held it ever since) and created a destination that attracts diners from across the country. In 2022, Mark was also honoured with a Trencherman's Award for Special Contribution.

Nestled in rolling hills between Tiverton and north Devon, the dining room offers views of the bucolic countryside from which many of the ingredients are sourced. Local produce is key for the couple and they've long supported regional farmers and growers, as well as developing the skills of college students looking to enter the industry.

Previously, Mark was head chef at The Waterside Inn at Bray in Berkshire so, as you'd imagine, the cooking is on point: elegant, beautifully executed and authentic to this countryside setting. Happily, The Masons Arms isn't somewhere to be reserved for special occasions as dishes are pleasingly priced.

Trencherman's tip: arrive in plenty of time to take a seat by the fire in the ancient bar and sip a G&T before heading into the restaurant for dinner.

Chefs Mark Dodson and Olivier Certain | **3 course dinner from** £50 | **Seats** 28

48 New Coast Kitchen

Contemporary cooking in Croyde

1 St Mary's Road, Croyde, Devon, EX33 1LF **01271 316026**
newcoastkitchen.co.uk

Given its position in Croyde village (the picturesque bonus to one of the UK's most highly rated surf beaches) you'd expect New Coast Kitchen's main draw to be its location – yet the cooking is by far the most compelling reason to visit.

Smart upscale food delivered in an attractively contemporary setting make this a great find – and a notable restaurant on the north Devon dining scene.

Dishes are crafted by a brigade dedicated to high-calibre cooking and the use of locally sourced ingredients. Feast on the likes of spring lamb saddle with braised belly, asparagus, aubergine, and new potatoes roasted in lamb fat and served with anchovy crumb.

Plant-based diners are also well catered for via creative compilations such as slow-roasted beetroot with blackberry and hazelnut, cashew cream and raspberry vinegar dressing. Whichever direction you take, you'll be well looked after by a friendly and knowledgeable front of house team.

Martin Baylis pilots the kitchen in his first head chef role. He worked at two AA rosette restaurants before moving to Devon in 2018 to hone his craft under James Mason at Michael Caines' Kentisbury Grange.

Kick off your visit on the turquoise bar stools and explore a cocktail list which pairs perfectly with appetisers such as fresh native oysters served with pickled apple, dill and chilli oil.

Trencherman's tip: the alfresco tables are lovely for casual feasting in the sun.

Chef Martin Baylis | **3 course dinner from** £60 | **Seats** 46

49 Number Eight

Award-winning tasting menus

49 Torrington Street, Bideford, Devon, EX39 2JD **01237 237589**

numbereightrestaurant.com

A slew of accolades (including Best Restaurant in the 2021 Trencherman's Awards and Best Restaurant in the 2020 Food Reader Awards) has cemented Number Eight's reputation as one of the region's most exciting restaurants.

As stalwarts of the hospitality scene in Cornwall, Joshua Jones and Chloe Wilks had plenty of industry experience to draw upon when, four years ago, they took the plunge and launched their own restaurant.

Going it alone was bold, but it paid off and Joshua's tasting menus have developed a fanbase of foodies who travel from all over the region to experience them. Joshua works alone in the kitchen, carefully sourcing top-notch produce for dishes such as cured local scallops with blood orange, while Chloe is the friendly face out front who looks after diners with calm efficiency and warmth.

In summer 2022, the restaurant moved from its unassuming location in a Bideford side street to a quayside venue in the north Devon town.

At the new space, guests get to experience delightful river views alongside Joshua's smart cooking, as well as the opportunity to sup in the chef's table room.

Chef Joshua Jones | **Tasting menu from** £80 | **Seats** 22

50 The Farmers Arms

Creative dining pub in the north Devon wilds

Woolsery, Bideford, Devon, EX39 5QS **01237 439328**

woolsery.com

This remarkable dining pub has cemented its reputation for casual but carefully crafted British pub food and a creative drinks experience.

Dine in one of three artfully rustic rooms or, in warm weather, bag a table in the courtyard. Wherever you sit, you'll feast on talented head chef Ian Webber's inventive reinterpretations of British classics.

Own grown, reared and foraged ingredients form the heart of the experience, with the house lamb and pork being particular highlights. In season, hogget is also available, while vegetables and herbs are picked daily year-round.

On Sundays, an extraordinary family-style lunch is served – simply tell the team if you're choosing the meat or veggie option and watch them deliver a smorgasbord of incredible edibles.

The pub, which serves uber-local ales, homemade cordials, inventive cocktails and an interesting selection of wines, is just one element of The Collective at Woolsery. It's joined by Woolsery Fish and Chips, Birch Farm and a village shop, while the creative reimagining of a Georgian manor house into boutique hotel Wulfheard Manor (and a next-gen bakery) are in development.

Trencherman's tip: don't worry if the satnav seems to be taking you to Woolfardisworthy – it's the older name for the village.

Chef Ian Webber | **3 course dinner from** £30 | **Seats** 50

51 Pattard Restaurant

Rural wonderland

Pattard Farm, Hartland, Devon, EX39 6BY **01237 441444**

pattardrestaurant.co.uk

This gastronomic gem may be hidden away in the green depths of Hartland's narrow lanes, but it's well worth journeying through remote Devon countryside to find it.

The hidden idyll is where chef Aaron Vanstone and a single sous chef craft elegant and contemporary dishes in the open-plan kitchen of an airy 24-cover barn conversion.

Local and seasonal produce is employed in menus that take a modern approach to classical British and French fine dining.

Beautifully presented dishes are complemented by an attractive rustic setting which is almost entirely crafted from wood, and complemented by accents from contemporary blue chairs, local

lino-cut prints and milk bottles (the barn was formerly a milking parlour) full of hedgerow flowers.

Aaron's partner Felicity Cook runs front of house, providing attentive service and wine recommendations to the diners who visit to feast on multifaceted dishes layered with seductive elements. Stuffed lemon sole, for instance, is paired with delectable surprises such as red orach and capers, wild dill pollen and blackened lemon puree.

On a warm day, a pre-dinner tipple or even lunch or dinner can be enjoyed alfresco on tables framed by lush verdant countryside and big blue skies.

Chef Aaron Vanstone | **3 course dinner from** £40.50 | **Seats** 24

52 The Riviera Hotel and Restaurant

Elegant dining in Regency Sidmouth

The Esplanade, Sidmouth, Devon, EX10 8AY **01395 515201**
hotelriviera.co.uk

This imposing establishment on Sidmouth's esplanade offers charming English seaside views and smart two AA rosette dining.

Attention to detail is the defining characteristic of chef Patrice Bouffaut's modern British menus, while the hotel's heritage adds traditional appeal. Not only has The Riviera Hotel been run by the Wharton family for over four decades, the seafood on its menu is supplied by a third-generation local fishing family.

Get into the glamorous spirit of the place by sipping a cocktail in the Regency Bar or lingering over a lunch of classic dishes out on the sunny terrace.

With echoes of the South of France and a prime position on the seafront, The Riviera makes an elegant base from which to explore Sidmouth, a resort described by John Betjeman as *'a town caught still in timeless charm'*. The late poet laureate declared Sidmouth to be one of the most delightful seaside destinations in England, and its public gardens, bandstands, putting greens and croquet lawns continue to attract those in search of relaxation and tranquil pleasures.

If you opt for a gourmet break, glorious sea views are to be enjoyed from many of the hotel's tastefully furnished rooms and you'll be impeccably well looked after. The establishment is known for its genuine welcome, traditional hospitality and excellent service.

Chef Patrice Bouffaut | **3 course dinner from** £45
Seats 80 | **Bedrooms** 26 | **Room rate from** £236

53 Lympstone Manor

Star-quality escapism

Courtlands Lane, Exmouth, Devon, EX8 3NZ **01395 202040**
lympstonemanor.co.uk

Lympstone Manor, Michael Caines' glamorous Devon retreat, has quickly established itself as one of the most desirable destinations for fine-dining enthusiasts in the UK.

In just five years, the award-winning hotel overlooking the Exe Estuary has become the epitome of comfort, exclusivity and luxury.

At the heart of the experience is Michael's Michelin-starred cooking which is artfully matched with wines from Lympstone's world-class cellar.

Guests get to choose from tasting and à la carte menus in one of three stunning dining rooms, each named after views across the estuary: Powderham, Mamhead and Berry Head.

Those staying the night can prepare for a sumptuous supper with a soak in their own outdoor bath (with views of the gardens and estuary) and an aperitif from the in-room gin tray. Post-dinner delights include a sundowner at The Pool House Restaurant & Bar while watching the fading embers of the day over the Haldon Hills.

The five-star country house hotel's other attractions include six shepherd's huts, beautiful suites and rooms, tennis courts and a sculpture garden. From 2023, guests will be able to raise a flute of Michael's own Lympstone Manor Cuvée crafted from grapes grown on his 11-acre vineyard. The first vintage, a Triassic Pinot Noir, is already available to sample on the wine list.

Chef Michael Caines MBE | **3 course dinner from** £155
Seats 60 | **Bedrooms and shepherd's huts** 27 | **Room rate from** £395

54 The Galley Restaurant

Topsham's cracking seafood spot

41 Fore Street, Topsham, Devon, EX3 0HU **01392 876078**
galleyrestaurant.co.uk

'The best of Devon on a plate' **is how the team describe their offering at this intimate Topsham find. It's a fitting description of The Galley Restaurant, which has long held a solid reputation for beautiful food and friendly yet efficient service.**

The latter is the result of maître d' Patrick's duties: he flits from table to table, offering a wine pairing recommendation here, a menu explanation there, all the time keeping the lively spirit of bonhomie well topped up.

The restaurant's location, a stone's throw from the River Exe, is the reason for The Galley's seafood specialism. The bountiful haul of local fish and shellfish is undoubtedly the star of the menu and, thanks to the ever-changing nature of the catch, the line-up of dishes is regularly revised. You could visit The Galley a couple of times a week and always find something new to feast on.

It's not all about piscatorial pleasure though, as the likes of pan-roasted sea bream and Prosecco-battered haddock are supported by locally shot game and Devon-grown veggies on a pleasingly restrained menu of five elegant starters and five classic mains, plus desserts.

Attractive decor, a lively buzz and the quirky setting in foodie Topsham complete The Galley experience.

Trencherman's tip: if you're staying in Exeter, The Galley is only a short train or taxi ride from the Devon capital.

3 **course dinner from** £32.50 | **Seats** 48

TRENCHERMAN'S

Guide
30

Sharp's®
BREWERY
ROCK · CORNWALL

Exceptional beer to match exceptional food

sharpsbrewery.co.uk

H

55 **The Lamb**

Destination dining in Longdown

Longdown Road, Longdown, Devon, EX6 7SR **01392 811100**

thelamblongdown.co.uk

Make the short journey from Exeter to the quiet village of Longdown to feast on local produce at welcoming country inn The Lamb.

While the setting is traditional, the food certainly isn't: chef proprietor Dolton Lodge takes a contemporary approach and crafts smart dishes from locally and ethically sourced ingredients such as Perridge Estate deer, Elston Farm lamb, Brixham scallops and Cornish cod. Meanwhile, seasonal tasting menus (available Thursday to Saturday) satisfy indecisive diners who are happy to sit back and let Dolton take the driver's seat.

The attractive à la carte dishes are fortified by pub favourites which also benefit from a dose of the chef's creativity – think honey-glazed gammon chop with lacy fried duck egg and triple cooked chips, and aged beef-short-rib burger with cheddar, tomato, lettuce, smoked burger sauce and fries.

Complete the relaxed rural encounter with a post-dinner tipple (there's a good selection of local spirits behind the bar) by the roaring log fire.

Trencherman's tip: pair a visit with a rural ramble in the surrounding verdant countryside.

Chef Dolton Lodge | **3 course dinner from** £31 | **Seats** 40

56 The NoBody Inn

Whisky galore at a classic dining pub

Doddiscombsleigh, Exeter, Devon, EX6 7PS **01647 252394**
nobodyinn.co.uk

This charming 17th-century inn in the rural Devon village of Doddiscombsleigh enjoys a solid reputation for excellent wining and dining.

Off the beaten track in countryside not far from Exeter, it's so tucked away you'd never just stumble across it. However, those in the know visit for the lovely cooking and incredible drinks collection: 240 whiskies and 30 wines by the glass, plus an impressive cellar of bottles from across the globe.

It's a dining spot for all seasons and in summer foodies make a beeline to the inn for lunch in the garden. However, The NoBody Inn is undoubtedly at its most atmospheric in the depths of winter when open fires, low ceilings, blackened beams and authentic interiors combine with the crackle of logs in the grate and the soft glow of candlelight.

If wine and whisky aren't your bag, you'll certainly find a spirit to seduce you – the orange notes of the house gin are a good place to start – as well as a sterling collection of well-kept ales and beers.

However, the pleasures extend way beyond those of the liquid variety and the crowd-pleasing cooking (crafted from a wealth of locally produced ingredients) deftly walks the line between smart and hearty. Ingredients such as local venison and fish from the Devon coast are treated with cheerful reverence.

Trencherman's tip: attractive guestrooms make The NoBody Inn a great spot for a gourmet getaway, solving the 'who'll be designated driver?' argument.

3 course dinner from £35 | **Seats** 45 | **Bedrooms** 5 | **Room rate from** £105

57 Gidleigh Park

Glorious country house hotel

Chagford, Devon, TQ13 8HH **01647 432367**
gidleigh.co.uk

Set amid 107 acres of gardens and woodland on Dartmoor National Park, Gidleigh has long been of note on the South West culinary map.

Current executive head chef Chris Eden's produce-led ethos results in refined plates built around flavour, which are skilfully laced with a dash of adventure and invention.

Dishes such as aged fillet of beef cooked over coals and served with smoked bone marrow, garlic and spinach deliver a heady treat for committed carnivores. Plant-based diners are equally spoilt by creations such as Vulscombe goat's cheese and spelt agnolotti with salt-baked onion, hazelnut and artichoke.

The experience at Gidleigh is so much more than good cooking, however. Diners are taken on a journey that begins with a glass of Champagne and exquisite canapés by a crackling fire in the sitting room, and continues with sommelier-picked wines paired to each course, followed by coffee and petits fours.

Oak-panelled dining rooms with views of the garden provide an elegant setting for Chris' creative cooking, while a terrace overlooking the croquet lawn is a pleasing alfresco option.

Trencherman's tips: although the bedrooms are beautiful, visitors don't have to stay the night to enjoy Gidleigh's mature gardens, a game of croquet, a round on the Peter Allis 18-hole putting course or fly fishing.

Sister Brownsword hotels and Trencherman's members The Slaughters Manor House, Buckland Manor, Minster Mill and The Bath Priory offer similarly exquisite experiences.

Chef Chris Eden | **3 course dinner from** £125
Seats 50 | **Bedrooms** 24 | **Room rate from** £360

58 Two Bridges Hotel

Destination dining on Dartmoor

Dartmoor National Park, Devon, PL20 6SW **01822 892300**

twobridges.co.uk

A Best Trencherman's Hotel

Consider this your tip-off on a great escape in the wilds of Dartmoor where, after a day spent exploring rugged countryside, you can hunker down for a sumptuous dining experience.

The cosy interiors of the 2022 Best Trencherman's Hotel are perfect in this moorland setting: roaring fires, grand paintings, polished brass and copper, and a well-stocked bar are just what you'd hope to discover after a day tramping over the hills.

However, it's not only ramblers and hikers who flock here for a taste of old-school conviviality (although you'll find a fair few in summer) as the rural hotel also enjoys a fine reputation for its food.

Talented executive chef Mike Palmer has built a loyal fanbase of foodies who visit for his creative cooking. Start your meal with a board of homemade breads and flavoured butters before indulging in an elegant multi-course menu. Dishes are carefully crafted with ingenuity and served in a charming panelled dining room with original stained-glass windows.

Fine wines complement the cooking, and the hotel often hosts wine-pairing dinners. The Two Bridges Devon cream tea is equally noteworthy – and best devoured fireside while the wind whistles outside.

Those looking to stay over will find comfortable bedrooms with four-poster beds and antique furniture.

Chef Mike Palmer | **3 course dinner from** £54
Seats 60 | **Bedrooms** 32 | **Room rate from** £109

S
H

FREE
HOUSE
AND
ROOM

59 The Bull Inn

Organic pub dining in Totnes

Rotherfold Square, Totnes, Devon, TQ9 5SN **01803 640040**

bullinntotnes.co.uk

In 2018, organic champion and ethical entrepreneur Geetie Singh-Watson took over the then crumbling Bull Inn. Her plan was to turn it into a destination where locals could gather for delicious food and visitors stay the night in sustainable comfort.

After a year of hard graft the vision was realised, and The Bull Inn quite quickly became a pillar of on-point organic dining for both the local community and beyond. Its popularity even saw it voted Best Dining Pub in the South West in the Food Reader Awards 2022, bolstering The Bull's slew of silverware which includes Best Eco Hotel in the UK and inclusion in The Times Top 100 Hotels.

Head chef Johnny Tillbrook utilises fantastically fresh produce – largely sourced from a cooperative of local and organic growers – in the creation of a daily line-up of dishes which are scribbled on blackboards. This menu is split into small and large plates, and guests are encouraged to order for the table and dig in, sharing style.

Fish from Brixham dayboats and meat from ethical farms supplement the soil-grown ingredients, so plates such as heritage tomatoes with labneh, herbs and croutons rub shoulders with barbecued sirloin topside with pickles and mustard mayonnaise.

The distressed-chic decor of the spacious dining room continues upstairs in the collection of guestrooms. Stay the night if you intend to explore the list of natural wines and the independent town of Totnes.

Chef Johnny Tillbrook | **3 course dinner from** £35
Seats 50 | **Bedrooms** 9 | **Room rate from** £120

60 The Angel – Taste of Devon

Relaxed fine dining in Dartmouth

2 South Embankment, Dartmouth, Devon, TQ6 9BH **01803 833488**

theangeldartmouth.co.uk

Elly Wentworth, former *MasterChef: The Professionals* finalist, continues to delight South West diners with her culinary mastery at this iconic Dartmouth restaurant. The Angel has an illustrious past and this spectacular setting is enjoying an exciting era under Elly's tenure.

The restaurant is a great example of relaxed fine dining at its best, and the team take as much care over guests' comfort as they do in the sourcing, cooking and presentation of delicacies such as roast diver scallops and Devon Red venison.

From the likes of rice cracker canapés with curried mayonnaise and caviar to beetroot tart with poppy seed goat's curd, beetroot jam and sorrel (served theatrically on a raised platter),

every minute detail is fashioned with artistry and an eye for presentation.

The puddings are equally intricate and include delights such as an indulgent "chocolate bar" with layers of lime caramel and pistachio.

Seats by the large picture windows offer lovely views over the harbour, so arrive early and explore the impressive drinks menu (which includes a superb wine list and notable local additions) while watching boats bobbing on the River Dart.

Trencherman's tip: if you want to see how Elly and team craft the exquisite dishes, book a table close to the open kitchen and spy on the culinary action.

Chef Elly Wentworth | **3 course dinner from** £80 | **Seats** 26

61 Andria

European dining in Dartmouth

5 Lower Street, Dartmouth, Devon, TQ6 9AJ **01803 833222**

andriadartmouth.com

Born in Paris to Italian parents and trained in the UK, Luca Berardino merely has to retrace his roots to find inspiration for the modern European menus of his Dartmouth restaurant.

Named after the Puglian town of his ancestors, Andria is where the talented chef turns his memories and food experiences into unconventional tasting menus and a daily line-up of carefully crafted small plates. Presentation is clean, simple and designed to let bold flavours shine.

Given its location in the smart harbour town of Dartmouth, it's no surprise that Andria's menus often swim with the likes of Brixham crab, local cod and hand-dived Torbay scallops. There's a good showing of local meat too, including Devon-reared beef, pork and lamb.

However, this is not a dining spot solely for carnivores. Vegetarians are also well catered for via a dedicated menu that features creative compilations such as Dawlish hen of the woods with parmesan cream, slow-cooked egg yolk and chives.

The pleasing food is accompanied by a great playlist, relaxed atmosphere and top-notch wines which include an impressive selection available by the glass.

Chef Luca Berardino | **3 course dinner from** £40 | **Seats** 32

62 Twenty Seven by Jamie Rogers

New-wave fine dining in Kingsbridge

9 Mill Street, Kingsbridge, Devon, TQ7 1ED **01548 288847**
27devon.co.uk

Jamie Rogers was always destined to captain an award-winning restaurant, having earned his stripes working in some of the South West's most prestigious kitchens.

It didn't take long for the accolades to start rolling in for the *MasterChef: The Professionals* semi-finalist. He was named South West Chef of the Year at the age of 23 and, a few years later, picked up the prestigious Trencherman's Best Newcomer Award for Twenty Seven by Jamie Rogers, his first solo venture (named in honour of his age at its inception). In 2021 he earned a Michelin plate for the Kingsbridge restaurant.

Produce is at the heart of the operation, and everything included on the inventive menus is sourced from within 25 miles of the restaurant. Dishes are designed to intrigue and delight, with ostensibly random collections of ingredients combined to create a symphony of colour, texture and flavour.

The best way to sample all this is to explore the multidimensional six-course tasting menu. Undertaking the matched drinks flight is a must too, as fortified wines and cocktails feature alongside interesting wines.

Trencherman's tip: arrive early to fully explore the cocktail list in the bar before dinner.

Chef Jamie Rogers | **3 course dinner from** £65 | **Seats** 40

63 Àclèaf

Precision plating at Boringdon Hall

Boringdon Hall Hotel, Boringdon Hill, Plymouth, Devon, PL7 4DP **01752 344455**
acleaf.co.uk

Grade II-listed Boringdon Hall Hotel may be steeped in history, thanks to its Elizabethan architecture and inclusion in the Domesday Book, but it's also home to this contemporary fine-dining restaurant.

Àclèaf is an intimate and romantic setting in which to sample the seasonal nine-course tasting experience from talented head chef Scott Paton.

'Dining at Àclèaf is interactive — a nine-course menu with twists and turns along the way,' is how Scott describes the experience. The focus is fully on ingredients, and the chef expends

serious energy sourcing the best produce to create his complex and unique dishes.

Hero ingredients on the seasonal menus include Devon crab, Dartmoor lamb, Highland wagyu beef and locally dived scallops, while vegetarian and vegan diners get their own tasting menus crafted from flavour-forward regional produce.

Scott's eye for exquisite design-driven plating and his talent for palate-pleasing combinations are complemented by an English-led wine flight.

Chef Scott Paton | **9 course tasting experience** £100
Seats 40 | **Bedrooms** 41 | **Room rate from** £200

64 Barbican Kitchen

Supper with spirit

60 Southside Street, Plymouth Gin Distillery, Plymouth, Devon, PL1 2LQ **01752 604448**

barbicankitchen.com

Well established as one of Devon's gourmet go-tos, Chris and James Tanner's Barbican Kitchen continues to deliver the gastronomic goods 16 years on.

Situated inside a historic building that's also home to the Plymouth Gin Distillery (and where the Pilgrim Fathers spent their last night before setting sail on the Mayflower), the location makes for an inspiring experience – even before you've sampled the cooking. The ancient stone of the harbourside building is complemented by contemporary styling to create a successful marriage of old and new.

A relaxed vibe sets up expectations for the smart-casual menu – which the team deliver in style. Dishes are built around locally sourced ingredients such as fish landed by Looe dayboats and meat from Philip Warren Butchers in Launceston. This fine fare is crafted into creative dishes such as lamb cutlets with shoulder terrine, crispy sweetbread, ratatouille and asparagus, alongside a line-up of modern British classics.

Committed carnivores will revel in the fruits of Barbican Kitchen's charcoal grill: West Country moorland beef, which has been dry aged for succulence, is seared over hot coals for flavour. Just choose a sauce and a starch, such as skinny fries or buttery mash, to accompany.

Plant-based visitors will be pleased by the superb selection of veg-centric dishes, all crafted using hyper-fresh ingredients from the surrounding Devon countryside.

Celebrating? Hire the private dining room which caters for up to 24 guests.

Chef Martyn Compton | **3 course dinner from** £26 | **Seats** 100

65 The Horn of Plenty

Intimate country house hotel

Gulworthy, Tavistock, Devon, PL19 8JD **01822 832528**

thehornofplenty.co.uk

This edge-of-Dartmoor country house hotel not only enjoys spectacular views across the Tamar Valley towards Bodmin Moor, it also deals in beautiful and inspiring food.

Head chef Ashley Lewis, who trained under the Roux brothers at The Waterside Inn at Bray, recently secured a third AA rosette for The Horn of Plenty restaurant.

The ambitious chef scours the Devon coast and countryside for quality ingredients from which to craft exciting menus. Refined yet unfussy dishes such as roast Devon beef fillet with confit onion, broccoli, carrot, wild mushrooms and red wine jus set the scene for an elegant gourmet experience.

Sit in the smart dining room or outside on the spacious terrace to drink in the luscious surroundings as you delight in spot-on service and excellent cooking. In 2020, the team at The Horn of Plenty rolled out a flurry of renovations including extensions of the bar, restaurant and alfresco dining areas, plus a colourful Moroccan-inspired refurb of the drawing room.

Mature gardens, beautiful rooms overlooking the moor and attractive furnishings make the country house a thoroughly charming spot for a rural retreat in this verdant corner of Devon.

Trencherman's tip: the ancient town of Tavistock is just a few minutes' drive away and Plymouth within easy reach. The splendour of the Tamar Valley, with its excellent walking, horse riding and mountain biking opportunities, is on the doorstep.

Chef Ashley Lewis | **3 course dinner from** £52.50
Seats 40 | **Bedrooms** 16 | **Room rate from** £130

66 Hotel Endsleigh

Refined elegance in the countryside

Milton Abbot, Tavistock, Devon, PL19 0PQ **01822 870000**

thepolizzicollection.com

Sister to Hotel Tresanton in St Mawes and The Star in Alfriston, East Sussex, this is the Devon contingent of the Polizzi family's trio of gorgeous hotels.

Located on the edge of Dartmoor, the Grade I-listed former residence of the Duke of Bedford enjoys sweeping views over its stunning gardens to the Tamar Valley. The scenes from the restaurant and lounge windows are particularly lovely – especially with a glass of local Sharpham Wine to hand.

Tempting diners' attention away from the rolling countryside is the clever cooking of head chef Thomas Ewings. Smart dishes such as lamb rump with faggots, potato terrine, shallot puree and summer vegetables do

justice to luscious local ingredients. The wood-panelled dining room – complete with roaring log fire and original features – makes a fitting backdrop to such splendid feasting.

Treat yourself to an overnight stay in one of the charming bedrooms or spacious Stable Suites and luxuriate in peaceful repose in this quiet rural setting, followed by a cracking country-house breakfast the next morning.

Trencherman's tip: amid the 100 acres of fairytale gardens, visitors may stumble upon a truly magical house which is paved floor to ceiling with shimmering shells.

Chef Thomas Ewings | **3 course dinner from** £62.50
Seats 40 | **Bedrooms** 19 | **Room rate from** £240

67 Lewtrenchard Manor

Historic splendour at the Manor

Lewdown, Okehampton, Devon, EX20 4PN **01566 783222**
lewtrenchard.co.uk

This family-run Jacobean manor house hidden away in rural Devon is a delicious place to dine and stay.

A visit is rather like stepping back in time, thanks to Lewtrenchard Manor's wood panelling, stucco ceilings, ancestral portraits, and the crackling logs lighting up the huge elegant fireplaces.

The house is steeped in history and was even mentioned in the Domesday Book. In 1626 it was bought by Henry Gould and remained in the family for many generations (eyeball the Gould clan over dinner – their portraits hang in the dining room). Then, in the 19th century, Reverend Sabine Baring Gould – who penned *Onward Christian Soldiers* – inherited the property and transformed it into the house it is today.

However good Baring Gould's taste in architecture, it's odds on he didn't have a chef who could create the kind of beautiful dishes that modern-day visitors experience. David Brown is Lewtrenchard's new head chef and he's busy crafting the next phase of the country house hotel's culinary reputation. He's got great raw ingredients to work with, including many freshly plucked from the kitchen garden.

Choose between à la carte or tasting menus and ensconce yourself in the panelled dining rooms, or book the Purple Carrot private chef's table experience with its flat-screen views of the kitchen action.

Chef David Brown | **3 course dinner from** £57.50
Seats 35 | **Bedrooms** 13 | **Room rate from** £180

68 Pyne Arms

Delicious Exmoor experience

East Down, Barnstaple, Devon, EX31 4LX **01271 850055**

pynearms.com

Delightfully rustic surroundings (proper pub decor, dark beams, wood burner, ancient wooden settles and locals propping up the bar) belie the contemporary culinary cleverness going down at the Pyne Arms.

Forget self-conscious styling; authenticity rules at this rural Exmoor gem. Hearty dishes such as unctuous slow-braised ox cheek with herby mash, and rib-sticking suet pudding feature alongside fresh local fish and gratifying burgers. Whatever you plump for, you can be sure of being well fed (and warmly welcomed) by owners Amie and Ellis Pannell.

The pair have hauled this hidden-away village pub into the 21st century through a menu of great cooking, an excellent local gin list, well-kept ales on tap – including the chocolatey Mena Dhu stout from Cornwall's St Austell Brewery – and friendly service. Their efforts won them Trencherman's Best Dining Pub in 2019.

Pyne Arms also has two contemporary guest bedrooms on site, so it's possible to turn supper into a mini-break on the edge of Exmoor. The opportunity to wake up in the verdant wilds and spend the day stomping over the moor, or exploring nearby National Trust property Arlington Court, before returning for a hearty supper and a pint at the bar is more than a little appealing.

Chef Ellis Pannell | **3 course dinner from** £28
Seats 60 | **Bedrooms** 2 | **Room rate from** £75

69 Broomhill Estate

Eclectic exuberance in north Devon

Broomhill Estate, Muddiford, Barnstaple, Devon, EX31 4EX **01271 850262**
broomhill-estate.com

Putting the 'art' into artisan dining is the ethos at the newly renovated Broomhill Estate on the edge of Barnstaple.

Set in the heart of a forest, the boutique art hotel and refined restaurant has long enjoyed a reputation for its magical contemporary sculpture trails and winding streams through acres of woodland and river meadows. However, its new owner Alex Kleiner has shaken up Broomhill and introduced a more eclectic vibe. Authentic Hollywood props such as the *Fight Club* soap, *Jumanji* board and an original *Predator* costume rub shoulders with artwork from artists of note such as Almuth Tebbenhoff, Andrew Stonyer and Jonathan Michael Ray.

The food's undergone a revolution too: it's now modern British in style and rooted in regional produce, including ingredients foraged from within the grounds of the estate. Menus celebrate and support local producers, so diners can expect to feast on the likes of Plaistow Mills trout, Crediton duck, Appledore mussels, Exmoor beef, Okehampton guinea fowl and seasonal vegetables from Broomhill's own smallholding.

Attractive plating coordinates artfully with the surroundings, while exciting pairings from a fabulous list of exclusively English wines provide oenophilic authenticity.

Trencherman's tip: seven gorgeous bedrooms with super-king-size beds (and inspired by cult classics, from *Clockwork Orange* to *Amélie*), provide an opportunity to explore this creative wonderland in depth.

Chefs Elio Debae and William Hickman | **3 course dinner from** £50
Seats 20 | **Bedrooms** 7 | **Room rate from** £180

70 Saveur

Parisian bistro vibes in Exmouth

9 Tower Street, Exmouth, Devon, EX8 1NT **01395 269459**
saveursrestaurant.com

You don't have to cross the Channel for Parisian bistro vibes and Euro-inspired cooking when you can make a seaside excursion to this Exmouth find. Tucked away on a pedestrianised street just off the main square, Saveur is the locals' best-kept culinary secret.

Chef patron Nigel Wright's menus change daily and, thanks to the restaurant's proximity to the ocean, there's a natural leaning towards fish and seafood in the modern, seasonal dishes. Nigel has a hotline to the fishmongers at Brixham Fish Market so only the freshest fish make it onto his European-influenced menus. Delight in the likes of crispy panko monkfish scampi with sweetcorn salsa, curry oil and coriander.

A range of specials, chalked up each morning, include the catch of the day. For pesca-phobes, there's locally reared beef, lamb and other seasonal Devon delicacies, as well as vegetarian and vegan options for plant-based diners.

Like the decor, the service is relaxed and welcoming, making this a très charmant find for both a casual lunch with friends and an intimate dinner à deux.

Trencherman's tip: catch the train from Exeter to make the most of the restrained but impressive wine list.

Chef Nigel Wright | **3 course dinner from** £36 | **Seats** 20

71 The Horse

Mediterranean surprises on Dartmoor

7 George Street, Moretonhampstead, Devon, TQ13 8PG **01647 440242**

thehorsedartmoor.co.uk

Step into The Horse, with its leather sofas, crackling fire and sociable atmosphere, to discover why it enjoys a cult following among locals and visitors to Dartmoor.

While the pub's pretty Moretonhampstead location and rustic vibe speak for themselves, it's the delicious Mediterranean-leaning menu that clinches the deal for food lovers.

At lunchtime, its fans head to the pub to sip award-winning ales and feast on specialities such as the hot-smoked salmon bagels with cream cheese and rocket.

In the evening, chef Nigel Hoyle lets his creativity fly in daily changing menus involving ingredients such as home-cured bresaola (Dartmoor beef topside cured for two weeks in red wine) and crisp arancini with Dartmouth Bay crab, lemongrass and chilli.

Alongside The Horse classics (River Exe mussels in local scrumpy and Dartmoor sirloin are favourites) trot signature pizzas, crisped to perfection in a custom-built oven. Twice-risen focaccia dough topped with all manner of seasonal specialities, from slow-braised wild rabbit to locally foraged wild garlic, provides yet further delight.

Chef Nigel Hoyle | **3 course dinner from** £22 | **Seats** 60

72 Mill End Hotel and Restaurant

Delicious Dartmoor dining

Chagford, Newton Abbot, Devon, TQ13 8JN **01647 432282**
millendhotel.com

Set in woodlands on the banks of the River Teign and with Dartmoor National Park on the doorstep, this former 15th-century flour mill is a delightful destination for walkers, dog-owners and discerning diners.

Follow a day out to nearby Castle Drogo, Fingle Bridge or the pretty market town of Chagford with a pre-dinner tipple in one of the comfortable lounges. Savour your sip as you gaze at beautiful riverside gardens or, in winter, the crackling log fire.

The daytime Lounge and Lawn menu is an opportunity to indulge in the likes of classic finger sandwiches, homemade sachertorte, and passionfruit and buttermilk pudding.

Dinner, by contrast, is a candlelit affair where head chef Laszlo Hegyi and team showcase locally landed seafood, South West cheeses, meat from nearby farms and moorland game. Everything, from bread to sauces, is produced in-house and fashioned into thoughtful dishes presented with flair.

Those wishing to prolong their stay at this historic house (a former residence of jet engine designer Frank Whittle) can choose from 21 rooms with views of the gardens, the wild glory of Dartmoor or the Teign River.

Trencherman's tip: the hotel is canine friendly and there are even special doggy dining areas, so there's no need to leave your pooch at home.

Chef Laszlo Hegyi | **3 course dinner from** £45
Seats 43 | **Bedrooms** 21 | **Room rate from** £120

73 The Dartmoor Inn

Smart moorland dining

Moorside, Lydford, Okehampton, Devon, EX20 4AY **01822 820221**

dartmoorinn.com

This country inn is a huge hit with savvy foodies on the hunt for sophisticated Dartmoor dining.

There are country inns aplenty for a pint at the bar after a moorland yomp but, for something smarter than post-hike pub grub, The Dartmoor Inn hits the sweet spot between homely bar and quality restaurant.

Jay Barker-Jones has led the kitchen since he and wife Tess (front of house) took over in 2019. His CV namechecks a number of award-winning kitchens while his focus at the inn is on crafting refined fare in a welcoming and unstuffy setting. The rabbit warren of a building has undergone extensive renovation, so the decor is as attractive as the food.

Jay's daily changing menu reflects both what's in season and produced locally. For a taste of Dartmoor, opt for starters like the tender wood-pigeon accompanied by jerusalem artichoke, hazelnut, mushroom and blueberries, and stellar mains like saddle of local venison.

The culinary offering includes an excellent seafood selection, too: whopping scallops are elevated with chorizo, pear and radish in the inn's most popular starter, while mains such as halibut with potato, bok choi, tomato, spring onion and punchy crab bisque are manna for fish fans.

Many dining destinations neglect quality at the bookends of a meal (i.e. bread and coffee) – but not here. Pleasingly bouncy homemade bread (baked in-house twice daily) and roasted-down-the-road speciality espresso from Okehampton's No.1 Coffee keep the standards up from first bite to final slurp.

Chef Jay Barker-Jones | **3 course dinner from** £32
Seats 60 | **Bedrooms** 3 | **Room rate from** £125

TRENCHERMAN'S

Guide
30

SW660

Experience the journey, discover the destination

southwest660.com

74 Gather

Hyper-local dining in Totnes

50 Fore Street, Totnes, Devon, TQ9 5RP **01803 866666**
gathertotnes.com

The term 'hyper-local' is often overused, yet the efforts of this Totnes restaurant justify the description: a co-op of local allotments stock the Gather kitchen with field-fresh organic vegetables, fish and seafood are landed at nearby Brixham and meat is reared within the county.

Talented chef Harrison Brockington leads a young team who use this glorious produce to create dishes that delight. And although the food is smart, the relaxed vibe and friendly service make it a go-to destination for all manner of occasions.

The kitchen team showcase their talents via full and half tasting menus – there's also a vegetarian version. The line-ups focus on flavour and provenance, and dishes such as duck with cherries, and woodruff custard tart are polished without being overly fussy.

The front of house team deliver excellent service with a light and friendly touch. An impressive drinks list is well thought out and, if you're indulging in the tasting menu it's worth splashing out on the wine flight.

Trencherman's tip: day trip to Totnes? The set lunch menu (Wednesday to Saturday) is excellent value, as is the prix-fixe early dinner menu (Tuesday to Thursday).

Chef Harrison Brockington | **3 course dinner from** £30 | **Seats** 25

75 The Bear and Blacksmith

Plot-to-plate dining in Chillington

Chillington, Kingsbridge, Devon, TQ7 2LD **01548 581171**

thebearandblacksmith.com

The Bear and Blacksmith specialises in dishes crafted from ingredients with the most incredible provenance: practically everything on the menu is grown, harvested or reared in-house.

Chef patron Malcolm Church wears a range of hats (including farmer, butcher and gardener) to deliver the Chillington inn's impressive plot-to-plate ethos.

Daily specials sit alongside a menu of classics fashioned around lamb from the pub's farm, free-range pork from its smallholding, house-reared free-range poultry, and veg from its gardens. Shellfish is sourced from local Salcombe fisherman Chris Roberts and the finest fish comes fresh from the Rex Down dayboats in Plymouth, while the grass-fed

Angus beef (hung for 30 days, minimum) is reared nearby by Jack Perry at Westdown Farm before being cut in the pub's butchery. The team also cure bacon, make sausages and smoke own-reared produce.

Such authentic ingredients speak for themselves and specialities such as 100 per cent grass-fed lamb cooked three ways – cutlet, leg steak and breast – are served with simple and delicious accompaniments such as homegrown squash and chard.

Malcolm likes to craft pastry as much as he relishes tending the veg patch, so leave room for one of the classic puds such as toffee apple tart topped with almond crumb and served with cinnamon ice cream.

Chef Malcolm Church | **3 course dinner from** £34 | **Seats** 42

76 The Jetty at Salcombe Harbour Hotel

Spectacular views and sparkling seafood

Cliff Road, Salcombe, Devon, TQ8 8JH 01548 844444

harbourhotels.co.uk/salcombe

There are few better views of Salcombe Estuary than those from The Jetty Restaurant at Salcombe Harbour Hotel. As the sun slips behind the horizon, the restaurant's terrace is a fabulous spot for drinking in the vista with a cocktail or glass of fizz to hand.

The panorama isn't The Jetty's only draw, however, as fresh fish and signature dishes from head chef Jamie Gulliford ensure the restaurant is permanently buzzing.

Thanks to a longstanding relationship with local fisherman, the latest market fish is always on the menu, alongside house favourites such as seafood curry, prawn and lobster bisque and a surf-and-turf platter.

The restaurant offers an all-day menu with the same sparklingly fresh options running from lunch to dinner, providing further alfresco dining opportunities for both residents and non-residents alike.

Of course, no excuse is required to stay the night. Many of the spacious rooms have views over the water, and all guests gain access to the sumptuous below-ground spa. And, as each room comes with decanters of gin and sherry, guests can raise a toast to a delicious south Devon staycation.

Chef Jamie Gulliford | **3 course dinner from** £38
Seats 96 | **Bedrooms** 50 | **Room rate from** £220

77 Harbour Beach Club

Chic beachside feasting

South Sands, Salcombe, Devon, TQ8 8LJ **01548 233456**
harbourhotels.co.uk

When, on high-summer evenings, Salcombe town overflows with tourists seeking a slice of south Devon coastal chic, those in the know head round the corner to South Sands to soak up the vibe without the hordes.

Harbour Beach Club, a gleaming new hotel, bar and restaurant overlooking the beach, is an insider's find for sipping cocktails on the deck and feasting on fabulous seafood in a slick dining room. It's also a pretty fabulous place to stay the night and wake to the sound of waves lapping the shore.

Yet, this isn't just a summer destination. In the colder months, it's a beautiful spot where visitors can snuggle up and watch storms roll over the headland or escape city life for quality time at the coast.

In the kitchen, head chef Daniel Foster works with group executive head chef John Pollard to create crowd-pleasing dishes which appeal to the wide variety of guests who seek out this waterside restaurant. Given the seaside setting, there's a natural leaning towards local fish and shellfish. Classics such as grilled lobster with garlic butter share menu space with contemporary creations like pan-fried sea bream with Asian broth, razor clams and saffron potatoes.

Pair your pick of the menu with something delicious from a lengthy wine list. There's a good showing from local Devon vineyards – a glass of sparkling Calancombe Estate Blanc de Noirs is an exquisite way to kick off an indulgent seafood feast.

Chef Daniel Foster | **3 course dinner from** £35
Seats 86 | **Bedrooms** 50 | **Room rate from** £275

78 Fletcher's Restaurant

Fine dining in the heart of Plymouth

27 Princess Street, Plymouth, Devon, PL1 2EX **01752 201523**

fletchersrestaurant.co.uk

Since opening in 2018, Fletcher's Restaurant has garnered a loyal following for its encore-worthy cocktails and showstopping cuisine.

Head chef Fletcher Andrews showcases a passion for quality local ingredients and vibrant earthy flavours in dishes such as braised venison with confit leek, truffle mash and cheese foam.

The chef is supported by a youthful front-of-house cast – led by Fletcher's fiancee Jessica Harkcom – who go out of their way to create a relaxed dining experience.

Glamorous pops of gold, low lighting and ambient music set the scene for cosy luxury; the restaurant is smart enough to be a special date-night destination but not so fancy as to put off those seeking a quick supper.

Fletcher's is also one to have in your little black book if you're planning to catch a show at nearby entertainment venues (it's in the heart of the city and just behind the Theatre Royal). Choose from pre-theatre menus, set meals and à la carte lunch and dinner line-ups. In summer, enjoy a long and lazy lunch in the light-flooded conservatory-style lounge.

Pudding lovers looking for a decadent finale wont be disappointed: the likes of vanilla mille-feuille with coffee parfait, candied pecans, vanilla ice cream and blood orange are worth making a song and dance about.

Chef Fletcher Andrews | **3 course dinner from** £45 | **Seats** 45

79 Salumi Bar & Eatery

Creative and contemporary

18 Millbay Road, Plymouth, Devon, PL1 3LH **01752 267538**

eatsalumi.co.uk

When it comes to flexible dining and timings, there are few chef patrons who put as much passion and energy into creating menus that work around modern customers' appetites and busy lives than Dave Jenkins.

Having already made a name for himself at Plymouth's Rock Salt Cafe and Brasserie, his contemporary approach to malleable menu creation has also been a huge hit at sister restaurant Salumi.

Working with head chef Jake Hardington, Dave's put together a mix-and-match foodie offering that's perfect for both feasting and nibbling – with something delicious to be enjoyed no matter the time of day.

Small plates, grazing plates and more substantial dishes (many with an Asian twist) have recently been complemented by new

pop-up Side Door @ Salumi – keep an eye on social for dates.

Centred around a fire kitchen in the garden, the pop-up serves breakfasts from the coals and lunches such as flame-cooked half-shell scallops with yuzu kosho and roasted seaweed. Turkish flatbreads, meat dishes, vegan specials and milk-jam iced coffee can be consumed in the heated and covered garden or as a takeaway.

Whether swinging by for a long and lazy sharing platter, lingering over Sunday lunch or hitting up a full feast of larger plates, diners can be assured that everything has been prepared with a field-to-fork philosophy. Sustainable produce includes mature grass-fed beef from Porsham Farm on the edge of Dartmoor and Salumi's own retired dairy cows.

Chefs Dave Jenkins and Jake Hardington | **3 course dinner from** £30 | **Seats** 50

80 The Fig Tree @ 36

French bistro vibes in Plymouth

36 Admiralty Street, Plymouth, Devon, PL1 3RU **01752 253247**
thefigtreeat36.co.uk

The daily menus at this neighbourhood bistro are a celebration of Devon's fruitful land and sea. Thanks to head chef Ryan Marsland's hotline to the region's finest suppliers, visitors can expect to feast on the freshest produce of the season – from just-landed River Exe mussels and Plymouth monkfish to Copplestone chicken and Creedy Carver duck.

Ryan utilises two decades of experience to create pleasingly pared-back dishes that sing with flavour. His Trust the Chef surprise menu (£33 for three courses) on Wednesdays and Thursdays is a fabulously affordable way to sample house specials such as pig's head terrine, lobster fries, and squid ink pasta. Round off an indulgent three courses

with the irresistibly silky brown butter crème brûlée served with strawberry sorbet and ginger crumb.

If the forecast is favourable, book one of the tables under the fig tree in the garden and kick off an alfresco supper with creative cocktails, plump olives and homemade bread. The restaurant is tucked away on a residential street a short walk from Royal William Yard, so it's perfectly positioned for a post-lunch stroll along the harbour.

Trencherman's tip: visit in the daytime to pick up takeaway treats at the deli, such as hot pork-belly sandwiches and Fowey mussels with warm bread and aioli.

Chef Ryan Marsland | **3 course dinner from** £37 | **Seats** 40

Cornwall

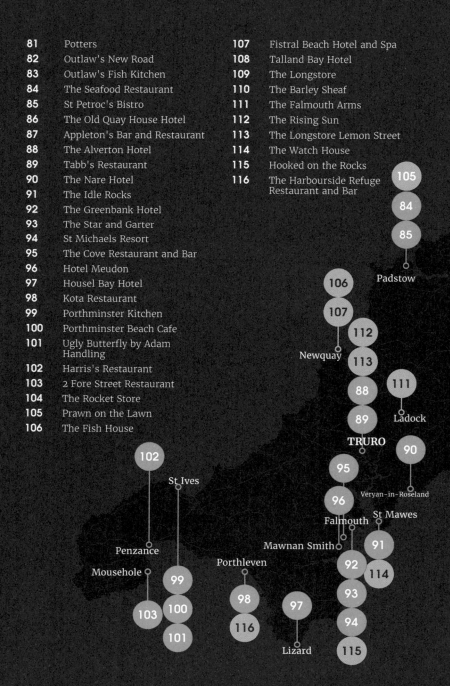

81

Bude

104

82

Boscastle

83

Port Isaac

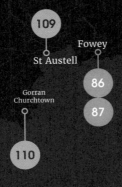

109

Fowey

Polperro

St Austell

86

108

Gorran
Churchtown

87

110

**Restaurants listed in the guide
correspond to the numbers plotted
on the map.**

All locations are approximate

81 Potters

Spellbinding cooking in Bude

2 Lansdown Road, Bude, Cornwall, EX23 8BH **01288 358466**
pottersbude.co.uk

The gastronomic reputation of the north Cornwall coast that centres on Rock and Padstow has inched up the Atlantic Highway with the launch (in the middle of the pandemic) of this Bude restaurant.

Chef owner Oly Clarke has worked at leading restaurants in the region, but this is his first venture as chef patron – and one he's undertaken with his wife Nikki.

The stars aligned when the pair discovered a substantial two-storey building in the middle of the seaside town, which they thoroughly refurbed to create an attractively understated frame for Oly's culinary art.

The restaurant is an evening-only affair. Choose between the tasting menu or go à la carte – which includes a couple of extra complimentary savoury courses flanking the starter, main and pud.

The menus are supremely seasonal and feature the likes of fresh local brill with a butter and brown shrimp sauce, served with asparagus and new potatoes. Vegetarians get to enjoy dishes such as wild garlic gnocchi with morels, asparagus and radish.

Oly has special charms in the pastry department so try not to fill up on the incredible bread and save room for the final course. Desserts such as a quivering slice of milky muscovado tart are guaranteed to cast a spell.

Chef Oly Clarke | **3 course dinner from** £60 | **Seats** 30

82 Outlaw's New Road

Fresh and creative in Port Isaac

6 New Road, Port Isaac, Cornwall, PL29 3SB **01208 880896**

outlaws.co.uk

Nathan Outlaw's eponymous restaurant in Port Isaac is in the midst of a new era in which precise and delicate tasting menus have been replaced by a more casual dining experience.

Unshackled from the activity required to maintain his restaurant's prestigious accolades (Restaurant Nathan Outlaw held two Michelin stars and scored 10/10 in *The Good Food Guide*), the chef is now cooking exactly the kind of dishes he loves to eat: high quality, local seafood crafted in simple ways to pay homage to the Cornish catch.

While unnecessary fripperies have been eliminated, Outlaw's is still the place to source excellently executed fish dishes.

The daily seafood set-menu is a celebration of Cornwall's bounteous coast and country, and demonstrates Nathan's ever-evolving creativity via a line-up of innovative dishes.

Striking views over the Atlantic vie for diners' attention with the excellent cooking and considered wine list (the team always have an on-point recommendation up their sleeve). This may be the latest incarnation of Outlaw's, but Nathan and his team's ethos – built on supporting local fishermen and sharing delicious food – remains unchanged.

A £3 donation to The Fishermen's Mission is included on every bill.

Chef Nathan Outlaw | **Set menu** £95 | **Seats** 20

83 Outlaw's Fish Kitchen

Casual cooking in a fishing village

1 Middle Street, Port Isaac, Cornwall, PL29 3RH **01208 881183**

outlaws.co.uk

With just five tables squeezed into a tiny 15th-century fisherman's cottage, Outlaw's Fish Kitchen is undoubtedly one of the smallest restaurants in the South West but, boy, does it punch above its weight.

Locally landed seafood is crafted with unfussy finesse into exquisite small plates and paired with a hand-picked collection of interesting wines. Hero dishes include Port Isaac lobster scampi with chilli jam and garlic mayonnaise, cured brill with red peppers, coconut and chilli, and whole dover sole with lemon and capers.

It's located by the slipway that leads the village fishing boats out into the green-blue waters of the harbour, and it would be hard to find a more picture-book-pretty setting in the whole of Cornwall.

The entire experience is attractive, intimate, casual and – thanks to Nathan's determinedly pared-back cooking which puts all the focus on ingredients – pleasingly rustic.

To get the vibe, imagine feasting with friends on a selection of sharing plates while quaffing a bottle of something crisp and delicious, and peeking through tiny windows at fishing boats chugging past.

Chef Nathan Outlaw | **Set menu** £80 | **Seats** 16

84 The Seafood Restaurant

Stein's Padstow flagship

Riverside, Padstow, Cornwall, PL28 8BY **01841 532700**
rickstein.com

The Seafood Restaurant is where it all began for Rick and Jill Stein. Their flagship restaurant, with its pleasing combination of smart-casual dining, ultra-fresh local seafood and global wines, paved the way for the subsequent additions to their foodie portfolio.

The ever-popular harbourside destination is under the care of head chef Pete Murt, a Padstow-born talent who previously worked as chef de partie and sous chef to The Seafood Restaurant's longstanding lead, Stephane Delourme.

Make the pilgrimage to sample classics from Rick's TV shows and books – from Indonesian seafood curry with cod, sea bass and prawns to tronçon of turbot with hollandaise sauce.

Dining at a table in the restaurant is delightful but, if you're only swinging by for a bite and a glass of something good, grab the opportunity to perch at the zinc bar and watch the action going on around you.

Those with a longing for a gourmet weekend in Padstow should check out the smart rooms above the restaurant or at Stein's other nearby establishments: St Edmunds House and St Petroc's Bistro.

Trencherman's tip: first trip to The Seafood Restaurant? Follow the crowd and order a bottle of something sparkling and the pièce de résistance: fruits de mer of fresh lobster, crab, mussels, whelks, clams, cockles, winkles, langoustines, scallops, oysters and razor clams.

Chef Pete Murt | **3 course dinner from** £45
Seats 130 | **Bedrooms** 16 | **Room rate from** £170

85 St Petroc's Bistro

Stein's French connection

4 New Street, Padstow, Cornwall, PL28 8EA **01841 532700**
rickstein.com

If you're looking for a stylish hideaway for lunch, dinner or an overnight stay just a short stroll from the bustle of Padstow harbour, this Stein bistro and boutique hotel is a lovely choice.

Jill Stein's relaxed styling gives the historic building a cultured air, creating a perfect setting for the bistro's classic French cooking.

Dry-aged steaks, the freshest Cornish seafood and a smart selection of wines seduce with their simple elegance. The menu changes regularly to reflect the micro-season, but an unwavering constant is the care with which quality ingredients are treated and the joy to be found in the unfussy dining experience.

In addition to its à la carte menus at lunch and dinner, the bistro runs a popular set lunch on weekdays which features three courses (such as fish and shellfish soup, moules frites and sticky toffee pudding) for a very keen £26.

Ten cosy rooms above the restaurant make a gourmet mini break in the seaside town a very seductive option.

Trencherman's tip: kick off dinner at sister establishment Ruby's Bar, where a creative compilation of cocktail choices is guaranteed to pique the palate for the dinner that follows.

Chef Mark O'Hagan | **3 course dinner from** £34
Seats 120 | **Bedrooms** 10 | **Room rate from** £170

86 The Old Quay House Hotel

Stylish waterside dining in Fowey

28 Fore Street, Fowey, Cornwall, PL23 1AQ **01726 833302**
theoldquayhouse.com

Once a refuge for sailors, the present-day incarnation of this whitewashed Victorian building is destination found for tourists heading to Fowey in pursuit of sea air, smart dining and a well-curated bar list.

The smart estuarine town, with its yachty vibe and winding narrow streets, offers excellent pottering and strolling opportunities for those who enjoy mooching about in design-led stores. However, being on the South West Coast Path, a serious stomp is also in the offing.

However you spend the daytime, there's nowhere like The Old Quay House Hotel's terrace – with exquisite views across the water – for sun-splashed dining on summer evenings. It's just the spot for feasting on locally sourced, high-quality seafood (such as torched mackerel and cured sea trout) against a tranquil backdrop of boats bobbing on the water. And, while diving into a dish of the freshest fish and shellfish might feel like the natural option in this location, piscatorial delights are accompanied by West Country meats, cheeses and veggies.

As the hotel houses a small but elegant Champagne bar – which also serves fabulous cocktails – the sensible option is to plump for an overnight stay in one of the bespoke bedrooms.

Spend a peaceful night's repose being lulled to sleep by the gentle clinking of the boats beyond your window, before refreshing yourself next morning with a gourmet breakfast of the highest order.

Chef Richard Massey | **5 course dinner from** £45
Seats 28 | **Bedrooms** 13 | **Room rate from** £200

87 Appleton's Bar and Restaurant

Italian-Cornish fusion in Fowey

19 Fore Street, Fowey, Cornwall, PL23 1AH **01872 228738**
appletonsrestaurant.com

Fowey has become a foodie hub in recent years, not least as a result of this creative restaurant which moved from Trevibban Mill to the centre of town just before lockdown.

Owners Andy (chef) and Lyndsey (front of house) Appleton have created an inspiring dining experience which combines modern European food with a good dose of Italian flair and lots of artisan Cornish produce.

Starters such as cured sea trout with fennel, radish, apple and sea buckthorn reference the lapping waters of the estuary just 100 metres away, while flat-iron steak with beef-fat potato, ox-cheek crocchette, cavolo nero and horseradish provide an edible link to the surrounding farmland.

Drinks are as inventive as the cooking and a strong list of Italian wines from most regions of the country rubs shoulders with Italian amari, liquors, bitters and vermouths – the latter fuelling Appleton's rep for its extensive Negroni list.

The restaurant is set over two floors, but the ground floor is the best spot to watch cocktails being crafted and the pasta machine churning out golden tagliatelle. The pasta is also available to buy – along with other interesting Italian produce – at the in-house deli.

Trencherman's tip: dogs are welcome, making a trip to Appleton's a fabulous reward at the end of a long walk along the coast path.

Chef Andy Appleton | **3 course dinner from £34** | **Seats** 60

88 The Alverton Hotel

Truro's luxury historic hotel

Tregolls Road, Truro, Cornwall, TR1 1ZQ **01872 276633**
thealverton.co.uk

Tucked away at the top of a winding drive and surrounded by verdant mature gardens, The Alverton is a surprising foodie find in Cornwall's capital city.

Ensconced on the sunny terrace with an exquisite cocktail to hand, you'd never believe you were just a ten-minute stroll from the bustle of the city. Consequently, the luxuriously refurbished bedrooms and suites make this Grade II-listed former convent a fantastic base from which to explore Truro and beyond.

Elegant and seasonal cooking comes courtesy of a team overseen by exec chef Nick Hodges. The intriguing menu features the best of both land and sea, with Nick's pick of the Cornish dayboats' catch sitting next to pasture-reared beef and locally foraged accompaniments.

Take a leaf out of the locals' book and order the surf and turf of fillet steak, garlic prawns, scallops, pont neuf potatoes, rocket, parmesan and saffron aioli.

Trencherman's tip: keep an eye on social media for details of The Alverton's events which include live music on the suntrap terrace.

Chef Ollie Wyatt | **3 course dinner from** £45
Seats 60 | **Bedrooms** 52 | **Room rate from** £139

89 Tabb's Restaurant

Truro's tiny treasure

85 Kenwyn Street, Truro, Cornwall, TR1 3BZ **01872 262110**
tabbs.co.uk

During the 16 years in which Tabb's Restaurant has fed locals and the tourists who flock to Cornwall's capital, the little restaurant has built a reputation as one of the city's most treasured gastronomic gems.

Those in the know make a booking well in advance for a table in the diminutive dining spot, not wanting to leave the opportunity of a guaranteed good dinner to chance.

Chef owner Nigel Tabb is a one-man band and creates everything from scratch each day. From freshly baked bread to chocolate truffles, it's all been crafted with care and attention to detail.

Despite the small size of this restaurant the cooking punches above its weight, and the result is a menu that showcases the region's most delicious and authentic produce. Seasonal dishes such as seared beef fillet with braised shin, parsnip mash and red wine jus are expertly executed and smartly presented.

While Nigel weaves his magic in the kitchen, partner Debbie Thorn conjures a relaxed and friendly atmosphere in the dining room. Thanks to the attention paid to diners' gastronomic pleasure, this intimate feasting spot is the antithesis of a chain-restaurant experience and more like having a private chef cook you dinner.

A substantial wine list accompanies the edibles and covers all corners of the globe. Kick off dinner in style with the exquisite Ruinart Blanc de Blancs Brut Champagne.

Trencherman's tip: Tabb's doesn't do lunch, but Nigel opens two Sundays a month for a very special roast.

Chef Nigel Tabb | **3 course dinner from** £27.50 | **Seats** 28

90 The Nare Hotel

Exceptional beachside hospitality

Carne Beach, Veryan-in-Roseland, Cornwall, TR2 5PF **01872 501111**

narehotel.co.uk

The Nare Hotel sits right by the beach, making it a fabulous destination for a leisurely stroll before lunch or dinner – or a gastronomic weekend away.

Whatever the duration of your visit, you'll discover two lovely dining options for foodies keen to indulge in the best of Cornish produce.

The nautically themed Quarterdeck Restaurant holds two AA rosettes and is renowned for its fresh seafood and succulent locally reared beef. Dine indoors amid maritime-inspired decor or head out to the deck for lunch in the sun.

Alternatively, The Nare Dining Room presents a classic fine-dining experience which is a traditional delight thanks to silver service, the hors d'oeuvres trolley, guéridon and flambé service. This is just the spot to feast on lobster drawn from the waters overlooked by the hotel.

Sea views come as standard in both restaurants, or you can get closer to the waves by booking a picnic aboard the hotel's motor launch. While this is a treat open only to residents, the exceedingly comfortable bedrooms (featuring sherry decanters and fresh flowers, and including an afternoon tea), make an overnight stay very appealing.

Don't miss the opportunity to start your evening in the bar where classic cocktails are accompanied by delicious nibbles and smart service.

Trencherman's tip: Sunday lunch at The Nare is an absolute treat – formal but unstuffy.

Chef Nick Lawrie | **3 course dinner from** £40
Seats 60 | **Bedrooms** 40 | **Room rate from** £312

91 The Idle Rocks

Idyllic retreat in St Mawes

Harbourside, St Mawes, Cornwall, TR2 5AN **01326 270270**
idlerocks.com

A Award for Creativity and Innovation

The Idle Rocks' waterfront location is a stunning setting from which to enjoy exceptional food and exemplary hospitality.

Trencherman's Award-winning Cornish chef Dorian Janmaat heads up the boutique hotel's kitchen and combines classic French culinary techniques with European influences from his travels.

Community is at the heart of The Idle Rocks, which the restaurant reflects by championing Cornish produce. The food is local and fresh, with daily deliveries procured from nearby MSC-certified fishermen.

The innovative menus cater for all dietary requirements, and signature dishes include the likes of butter-poached plaice with crab risotto, courgette and saffron velouté, and miso-glazed aubergine with bulgur wheat salad. Desserts are simple and elegant – think Cornish strawberries and tonka bean brûlée.

Start your visit with a cocktail on the terrace to soak up the tranquil views across St Mawes harbour. While those lucky enough to be staying at the Relais & Châteaux hotel get to gaze at rooms that fuse traditional coastal culture with contemporary design.

There's also a new treatment room – The Reef Knot Retreat – where guests can reset mind, body and spirit with a range of therapeutic treatments.

Trencherman's tip: request a Grand Seaview Room with a window-side tub so you can soak while watching sailing boats in the bay.

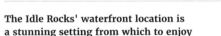

Chef Dorian Janmaat | **3 course dinner from** £85
Seats 50 | **Bedrooms** 18 | **Room rate from** £265

92 The Greenbank Hotel

Harbourside dining in Falmouth

Harbourside, Falmouth, Cornwall, TR11 2SR **01326 312440**
greenbank-hotel.co.uk

Falmouth is awash with decent places to eat but, for a stylish base where you can dine amid eye-catching interiors and harbour views, The Greenbank Hotel is wonderful.

The smart hotel delivers relaxed vibes and sophisticated cooking at the Water's Edge restaurant, which deals in creative fine dining crafted from local ingredients.

As the water laps the slipway wall below the hotel, it's natural to plump for fish and shellfish. Happily, plenty of dishes are crafted around the local fishermen's catch, as well as other examples of prime regional produce.

The adjoining Water's Edge bar is another fabulous spot from which to watch the boats bobbing as you indulge in one of the creative cocktails. On warm evenings, sip your tipple outside on the terrace.

Contemporary bedrooms make this an excellent base for a foodie trip to Falmouth. With the town's National Maritime Museum, Pendennis Castle and the South West Coast Path to explore, as well as a host of quirky independent shops and the opportunity to take a passenger-ferry trip to St Mawes, an overnighter could easily turn into a week-long gourmet getaway.

When you want to switch up the elegant dining, head below deck to the hotel's pub, The Working Boat, to sink a Cornish craft beer and tuck into hearty fare such as ale-battered fish and chips, Cornish crab doorstop sandwiches and surf-and-turf burgers.

Trencherman's tip: visit sister hotel The Alverton in Truro for more foodie adventures in historic horticultural surroundings.

Chef Bobby Southworth | **3 course dinner from** £45
Seats 60 | **Bedrooms** 61 | **Room rate from** £139

TótalPróduce

Suppliers of fresh, quality produce

totalproducelocal.co.uk

93 **The Star and Garter**

Contemporary and casual

52 High Street, Falmouth, Cornwall, TR11 2AF **01326 761441**

starandgarterfalmouth.co.uk

If there was a Trencherman's Award for the restaurant with the most surprising view, The Star and Garter would win every year.

From outside, the ancient pub on Falmouth High Street looks smart but unassuming. Walk past the cosy bar, however, and the expansive panoramic windows wrapping round the back wall reveal an incredible vista across the historic harbour.

Cosy banquette booths lining the window are very popular, and there's something rather special about eating sparklingly fresh fish while watching boats putter by below. Locally caught seafood is always on the menu, but the confident kitchen team also love to cook Cornwall-reared meats and were early adopters of the nose-to-tail philosophy.

The team prepare everything in-house and their skills include butchery, smoking and curing; they also cook over hot coals.

A hyper-seasonal approach means the menus change daily, although hero dishes such as chargrilled market fish with Isle of Wight tomatoes, tarragon, burnt hispi cabbage, aioli and ciabatta crumb, and aged moorland hanger steak with bone marrow butter, pickled onion rings and chips are popular staples.

Trencherman's tip: get a second helping of the wow-factor views from one of the three contemporary apartments available to rent above the pub.

Chef Robert Bunny | **3 course dinner from** £30
Seats 60 | **Bedrooms** 4 | **Room rate from** £170

94 St Michaels Resort

Feel good in Falmouth

Gyllyngvase Beach, Falmouth, Cornwall, TR11 4NB **01326 312707**

stmichaelsresort.com

This smart resort, which overlooks the azure waters of Gylly Beach, is an oasis of subtropical splendour in the foodie hub of Falmouth.

Guests will find endless opportunities to entertain themselves by wandering through lush gardens, lazing in the largest hydrothermal pool in the South West, being wrapped in seaweed in the spa or burning off calories in the high-calibre fitness centre. And that's even before factoring in the delights of sea swimming and paddleboarding on a beach which is practically at the end of the drive.

Two restaurants offer yet more choice and diversion, so guests barely need venture beyond St Michaels' perimeter. Brasserie

on the Bay specialises in locally caught and reared ingredients cooked on the grill, while The Garden Kitchen offers more casual dining with the likes of wood-fired pizza and nutritious salads.

A stool at the island bar is the perfect place to start an evening of feasting; dip into the cocktail menu and chat to the friendly front-of-house crew as you soak up the fun holiday vibe.

Trencherman's tip: check out St Michaels' latest development, The Liner. Its stylish beachside residences are ideal for self-catered breaks and come with all the benefits of a stay at the main resort.

Chef Darren Millgate | **3 course dinner from** £45
Seats 80 | **Bedrooms** 92 | **Room rate from** £75

95 The Cove Restaurant and Bar

Michael Caines' seaside spoils

Maenporth Beach, Falmouth, Cornwall, TR11 5HN **01326 251136**
thecovemaenporth.co.uk

Just a stone's throw from the foodie hub of Falmouth lies Maenporth Beach, a beautiful bay of golden sand and turquoise water that's also home to Michael Caines' relaxed coastal eatery.

The Cove takes full advantage of its glorious setting: floor-to-ceiling windows and a spacious terrace treat diners to uninterrupted views of the beach and across to the Roseland Heritage Coast. Heaters, blankets and a retractable roof allow guests to enjoy the alfresco experience all year round.

If you've tried Michael's Michelin-starred cooking at Lympstone Manor (his flagship manor house hotel and restaurant near Exmouth), you'll recognise his style, flair and flavours in the Signature Tasting Menu which features a number of the chef's hero dishes. The seven-course seasonal feast can be paired with the team's picks from the wine cellar for an unforgettable evening of wining and dining.

While the tasting menu is a draw, the relaxed all-day and specials menus are especially popular with locals, day-trippers and families. Michael's passion for fresh, local and seasonal produce is transformed into dishes such as pan-fried fillet of red mullet with wild mushroom gnocchi and lobster and fennel emulsion. Desserts such as a dark chocolate sphere with pistachio ganache, freeze-dried raspberries and chocolate sorbet are as delicious to admire on the plate as they are to eat.

With cooking this good, a day out to Maenporth for sand, sea and exquisite sustenance is a no-brainer.

Chef Michael Caines | **3 course dinner from** £45 | **Seats** 80

96 Hotel Meudon

Subtropical escapism

Mawnan Smith, Falmouth, Cornwall, TR11 5HT **01326 250541**
meudon.co.uk

Set in nine acres of subtropical gardens and overlooking the crystal-blue waters of the Atlantic, Hotel Meudon makes it easy to believe you're somewhere rather more exotic than the UK.

The recently refurbished hotel is located a short walk along the South West Coast Path from the beaches of Maenporth and Swanpool. It's also close to the foodie hub of Falmouth yet feels a world away from the hustle and bustle.

Enjoy an early-morning dip at the secluded beach, take a leisurely stroll around the grounds or luxuriate in afternoon tea in the second-floor conservatory while drinking in views of the coast.

With an award-winning restaurant on site, visitors don't even need to leave this little Eden for dinner. Restaurant Meudon serves elegant dishes which utilise the best of the local fishermen's catch, alongside Cornwall-reared meats and local vegetables.

Expect to feast on the likes of Cornish stone bass with spiced dal puree, baby spinach and lime butter sauce, followed by delicious desserts such as morello cherry soufflé with vanilla cream.

It's worth making time for a drink in Freddie's Bar before dinner. Its oxblood-hued walls, rich velvet furnishings and burnt-gold features create an inviting setting for cocktail hour.

Chef Charlotte Vincent | **3 course dinner from** £49
Seats 60 | **Bedrooms** 29 | **Room rate from** £119

97 Housel Bay Hotel

Divine dining and views

Lizard, Helston, Cornwall, TR12 7PG **01326 567500**

houselbay.com

Perched on nature's edge, the most southerly hotel on mainland Britain offers the prospect of being immersed in the wild beauty and drama of the Lizard Peninsula.

Start by sipping a cocktail from Marconi's Bar, either in the garden or by the open fire. Then head into Joseph Fallowfield's eponymous restaurant to enjoy creative clifftop cuisine that reflects the seasons and stunning landscape.

Ingredients, sustainably sourced from within a 25-mile radius of the hotel, include lamb that's grazed the fields of the farm next door and fish landed by the Cadgwith Cove boat (which can often be spotted from the garden).

'We create menus based around these fantastic suppliers,' says Joseph. *'It's much easier to create incredible food when you begin with incredible components.'*

Alongside the à la carte options, Joseph creates five-course tasting menus which take diners on a culinary tour of Cornwall. Occasional supper clubs also feature.

Sister restaurant The Terrace is another fantastic find, and perfect for relaxed dining or afternoon tea overlooking the bay.

The hotel's all-year-round charm is best experienced by staying in one of its 24 guestrooms, which each offer a unique view of the peninsula. Take it as an opportunity to switch off, reconnect with nature and ramble the coast path.

Chef Joseph Fallowfield | **3 course dinner from** £45
Seats 32 | **Bedrooms** 24 | **Room rate from** £85

98 Kota Restaurant

Award-winning fusion dining

Harbour Head, Porthleven, Helston, Cornwall, TR13 9JA **01326 727707**

kotarestaurant.co.uk

This Porthleven gem is the flagship restaurant of *Great British Menu* veteran (and previous Trencherman's Award for Special Contribution winner) Jude Kereama.

A cracking selection of seafood (Kota means 'shellfish' in Māori) takes centre stage at the harbourside venue – try the Rockpool for a smorgasbord of pan-fried hake, crab ravioli, Cornish mussels, tiger prawn, vegetable dashi broth and seaweed.

Jude's creative menus utilise top-notch local produce which shines when married with the vibrant flavours inspired by his travels around the globe, his Cornish fishing village home and Chinese-Malay and Māori heritage.

Book an overnight stay in one of the three bedrooms with views over the harbour and take full advantage of the tasting-menu wine pairings. Then, next day, trot over to sister bar-kitchen Kota Kai for a laid-back lunch of small plates such as Singapore soft-shell-crab bao buns with seaweed mayo and mango, and Korean fried cauliflower with gochujang, chives and leaves.

Chef Jude Kereama | **3 course dinner from** £35
Seats 32 | **Bedrooms** 3 | **Room rate from** £110

99 Porthminster Kitchen

Contemporary bistro by the beach

Wharf Road, St Ives, Cornwall, TR26 1LG **01736 799874**
porthminster.kitchen

This is the second restaurant in the feted Porthminster Collection, which includes Porthminster Beach Cafe and Porthgwidden Beach Cafe.

Like its sister establishments, this St Ives restaurant excels in serving top-quality Cornish seafood in a lively and fun coastal setting. Its location above the hustle and bustle of the town's harbour provides an awesome spot from which to watch fishing boats return with their catch, while tucking into a sample of the day's haul.

Classic house dishes include seafood linguine with crab, mussels, prawns, lemon and chilli, and fresh local fish such as roasted cod fillet with truffle mash, broccoli, pancetta, mushrooms and red wine sauce.

Porthminster Kitchen is not entirely about the fish and seafood, however, and visitors will find the menu meanders beyond the piscatorial to provide plenty to pique the appetites of both plant-based diners and keen carnivores. The restaurant also enjoys a great reputation for its cracking Sunday lunch.

Clean lines, rustic wood flooring, stainless steel, industrial lighting and fresh white tiles lend a contemporary vibe that lets the food do the talking.

Chef Daniel Banfield | **3 course dinner from** £50 | **Seats** 42

100 **Porthminster Beach Cafe**

Beachside feasting in St Ives

Porthminster Beach, St Ives, Cornwall, TR26 2EB **01736 795352**

porthminstercafe.co.uk

A Best Trencherman's Restaurant

Those who hanker after salty sea air and ocean views as an accompaniment to their gourmet encounters would be hard pressed to find many locations that deliver the goods as well as Porthminster Beach Cafe.

The bright white and wood dining room and heated outdoor terrace make it a winner all year round – and a breath of fresh air for those who despair at the winter shutdown of so many seaside dining spots.

The team have garnered a sterling reputation for exquisite dishes with Asian and Mediterranean influences which shine a light on the freshest seafood, garden-grown produce and foraged coastal ingredients.

House dishes include comforting smoked haddock chowder, fragrant Indonesian monkfish curry, and classic Cornish moules marinières, although head chefs Mick Smith and Edward Lee Wilson like to switch things up and change the menus each season.

As popular with locals as it is with discerning tourists, the coastal destination is open for all-day dining so, if you can't score a table in the evening, brunch or lunch are tempting options. Kickstart a day exploring the South West Coast Path by tucking into a plate of hot smoked salmon, poached eggs, fried halloumi chips and garlic aioli.

Chefs Mick Smith and Edward Lee Wilson | **3 course dinner from** £50 | **Seats** 100

Photo: John Hersey

H

101 Ugly Butterfly by Adam Handling

Sustainable local luxury

Carbis Bay, St Ives, Conrnwall, TR26 2NP **01736 805800**
uglybutterfly.co.uk

'There's no such thing as an ugly butterfly in the same way as there is no such thing as food waste' is the philosophy that weaves through chef Adam Handling's restaurant and bar at Carbis Bay. The dining experience is built on an ethos of sustainability and zero waste.

At this stunning seaside venue (one of Adam's trio of restaurants which include Frog in Covent Garden and The Loch & The Tyne in Old Windsor), his menus are executed by head chef Connor Blades who started working with Adam when he was just 15 years old.

Five- and seven-course menus (both vegan and non-vegan, and with optional wine flights) utilise the freshest locally reared and landed ingredients and deliver them in dishes such as St Enodoc asparagus with beach herbs and pilchard, and salt-aged lamb with morels and wild garlic. Any trims and off-cuts not used in the production of main dishes are employed by the Ugly Butterfly Bar team in the creation of delicious drinks and bar snacks.

Seductively creative plating is paired with the aesthetic delights of a contemporary restaurant with wrap-around views of the bay.

Trencherman's tip: start your visit with a platter of native oysters – three crispy, three fresh with all the trimmings – and a glass of Krug Champagne.

Chef Connor Blades | **5 course tasting menu** £100 | **Seats** 65

102 Harris's Restaurant

Perennial Penzance favourite

46 New Street, Penzance, Cornwall, TR18 2LZ **01736 364408**

harrissrestaurant.co.uk

Harris's Restaurant is something of a foodie institution in the seaside town of Penzance and this year celebrates the astonishing achievement of 48 years in the *Michelin Guide* and 30 years in *Trencherman's*. There are very few restaurants that can make that claim so, if you've never visited, it's worth swinging by to taste a slice of Cornish dining history.

The family team who run this bijou gem pride themselves on only cooking fish that's been landed that morning just across the bay in Newlyn, so diners can rest assured they're feasting on the freshest seafood. The same goes for shellfish: classic serves such as crab florentine and whole Cornish lobster do justice to the fishermen's haul.

While feasting on lobster and dover sole feels absolutely authentic by the coast, committed meat-eaters can also enjoy beautifully crafted dishes made from local meat and game. Favourites such as loin of venison feature on the menu of well-crafted classics and are definitely worth steering towards.

Save space so you can finish your three-course feast with one of the delicious desserts – such as chocolate torte with vanilla and amaretto sauce and blackcurrant sorbet – for which Harris's is known and loved.

Trencherman's tip: this elegant restaurant is situated in a fairly unassuming street so make the effort to track it down and, as it's not huge, be sure to book.

Chef Roger Harris | **3 course dinner from** £38 | **Seats** 20

103 2 Fore Street Restaurant

Bistro chic in Mousehole

2 Fore Street, Mousehole, Penzance, Cornwall, TR19 6QU **01736 731164**
2forestreet.co.uk

2 Fore Street is a relaxed gourmet gem right on Mousehole's harbourfront.

Sit inside and drink in the stunning views across Mount's Bay or, if it's sunny, head to the secluded courtyard garden. The alfresco area has its own microclimate, so treat yourself to a glass of chilled fizz and a dish from a menu of classics – the signature crab soufflé or local fillet steak with béarnaise sauce are good calls.

Only the freshest Cornish seafood, as well as locally sourced meat and veggies, makes its way onto the menus of Raymond Blanc-trained chef patron Joe Wardell.

While this slipway-side dining spot is a real find for dinner, those heading to the beach opposite are welcome to swing by for morning coffee or lunch. Brunch is an attractive proposition, with hero dishes such as toasted brioche with crispy smoked bacon and fried eggs showcasing top-notch local produce.

If you're looking to make a mini-break of it, check out The Boatwatch, the restaurant's cosy apartment on the harbour. With its maritime decor, wood-burning stove and open-plan living area, it's rather special.

Trencherman's tip: grab goodies to go from the deli shop which stocks St Ives Bakery treats, Freehand coffee, ice cream by Moomaid of Zennor and wine from Enotria&Coe.

Chef Joe Wardell | **3 course dinner from** £42 | **Seats** 34

104 The Rocket Store

Cornish seafood with an Asian twist

Boscastle Harbour, Boscastle, Cornwall, PL35 0HD **01840 250310**
therocketstore.co.uk

Listening to the lap of water and sniffing lunch on the salty air are just two of the pleasures of dining alfresco at this bijou Boscastle restaurant.

Nestled under green hills and tucked into the side of the characterful Cornish harbour, the charmingly rustic and intimate dining space offers a fish-focused menu with exciting twists of Asian flair.

A succession of gorgeously presented daily dishes parade from the open-plan kitchen, all crafted with a commendable attention to flavour. Prepare yourself for the likes of Porthilly oysters infused with a fiery chilli kick and sweetened with apple, hand-dived scallops lavished with seaweed butter, and butterflied mackerel accompanied by the gratifying tang of a Thai nahm jim sauce.

Friendly service, atmospheric music, a young ambitious team and a mix of natural and classic wines make The Rocket Store a restaurant worth making a detour to experience. Head chefs Freddie Woodruff and Alex Key have access to some of the best ingredients on the Cornish coast (including from their Boscastle farm Trebiffen and fishing boat Rene) which feature heavily on their menus.

Be sure to take along a group of seafood-loving co-conspirators to help you demolish the sharing plates, and keep an eye on the blackboard for specials based around the latest catch.

Chefs Freddie Woodruff and Alex Key | **3 course dinner from** £50 | **Seats** 40

105 Prawn on the Lawn

Spankingly fresh seafood

11 Duke Street, Padstow, Cornwall, PL28 8AB **01841 532223**
prawnonthelawn.com

One of Cornwall's most talked about seafood restaurants, Prawn on the Lawn actually started out in 2013 as a tiny fishmonger and seafood bar in Islington. The original venue was a such a hit that founders Rick and Katie Toogood decided to open a second site at the source of their impeccable produce: Padstow.

Their menus are dictated by what the Cornish fishermen land each morning, so no two visits to this bijou seafood bar are ever quite the same. Working closely with head chef Eddie Thomson, Rick favours sustainable fish and shellfish species and supplements the day's catch with hyper-fresh veg from Ross Geach of Padstow Kitchen Garden.

In 2020, the Padstow restaurant relocated to Trerethern Farm (on the outskirts of town) for the summer and the residency was such a success that it has continued ever since. From April to October, seafood lovers flock to the covered alfresco tables to feast on small plates, shellfish platters, oysters and whole fish.

Delicious dishes – think crispy chilli monkfish with pickled cucumber; sardines with feta, dill, mint and olive oil; and seared tuna with soy, mirin, spring onion and chilli – are complemented by local wines from Trevibban Mill (just a stone's throw away) and beers from Padstow Brewing Company.

Chefs Rick Toogood and Eddie Thomson | **3 course dinner from** £50
Seats 26 (Padstow town), 62 (Prawn on the Farm)

106 The Fish House

Seafood by the surf

Unit 5, International Surf Centre, Headland Road, Newquay, Cornwall, TR7 1HY **01637 872085**

thefishhousefistral.com

The South West isn't short of decent seafood restaurants, but to feast on the freshest catch while overlooking the big blue in which it swam takes the experience next level.

At The Fish House in Newquay, guests gaze out over Fistral Beach, watching surfers bob in the rolling waves, while tucking into some of the best seafood Cornwall has to offer. The family-run restaurant may be small in size, but its location and reputation for fantastic food has made it a big-hitter in the popular holiday destination.

Chef owner Paul Harwood knows a thing or two about turning seafood into star-quality dishes: before establishing The Fish House he worked for Rick Stein for over a decade.

His menus reflect both the skills he picked up at the Stein restaurants and his travels chasing big waves and big flavours.

The menus change depending on the local catch, but there is usually a selection of sharing boards to start – most notably the seafood medley which includes the likes of crispy squid, piquillo peppers with salt cod, crab cakes, tempura prawns, tiger prawns with sweet chilli, and bouncy homemade focaccia.

Main courses are a globetrotting collection of Paul's favourite finds. Feast on the likes of Indian fish curry, seafood risotto, Balinese-style monkfish, and crab and tiger prawn linguine.

Chef Paul Harwood | **3 course dinner from** £34.40 | **Seats** 28

Fistral Beach Hotel and Spa

Surfside glamour

A — Best Bar List

Esplanade Road, Newquay, Cornwall, TR7 1PT **01637 852221**
fistralbeachhotel.co.uk

This grown-ups-only hotel and restaurant in Newquay has a luxury resort vibe thanks to its incredible views, contemporary styling and rock-star extras.

There's no compromise if you swap the south of France for the Cornish coast and a visit to Fistral Beach Hotel and Spa. Overlooking the beach, the bar and restaurant's panoramic windows offer guests rolling coverage of the surfers riding the waves below. Spacious balconies in sea-view rooms provide yet more opportunities to watch the action.

After a relaxing day being pampered in the Fistral Spa, kick off the evening with drinks in the Bay Bar. The experienced team, who scooped Best Bar List in 2022 Trencherman's Awards, craft signature cocktails (try the Champagne Margarita) and serve local craft beers.

Dinner at the beautiful Dune Restaurant puts guests in the capable hands of head chef Daniel Kerr. He's spent much of his career in Cornwall so is well acquainted with seasonal Cornish produce and the best local suppliers. His smart menus put fabulous ingredients front and centre in dishes that flirt with Asian and Middle Eastern flavours.

The five-course tasting menu (with optional wine flight) is the best way to sample his ambitious cooking in creations like teriyaki mackerel with tartare, pickled cucumber and wasabi. There's also a vegan menu which goes above and beyond the usual to provide plant-based diners with creative options.

Chef Daniel Kerr | **3 course dinner from** £45
Seats 50 | **Bedrooms** 71 | **Room rate from** £175

108 Talland Bay Hotel

Escapist coastal dining

Porthallow, Looe, Cornwall, PL13 2JB **01503 272667**
tallandbayhotel.co.uk

Perched on a secluded stretch of coastline, this luxury hotel is in an ideal spot for those wishing to experience the true spirit of Cornwall, without the summer hordes.

A sense of 'getting away from it all' makes a visit to this hidden delight a wholly restorative experience. Ensconce yourself in the lush subtropical gardens with a Talland Bay No.1 gin: Cornish spirit crafted with pines and botanicals grown in the grounds. Then indulge in head chef Glen Merriot's French-influenced dishes in the fine-dining restaurant or sea-view conservatory.

With blue skies above and lapping waves below, the clifftop hideaway is the perfect backdrop for Glen's authentically Cornish cooking. Seasonal bounties like fresh fish from Looe dayboats, meat from Philip Warren Butchers and dairy from Rodda's Creamery inspire the chef's creativity and take centre stage in simple-yet-delicious compilations.

If you want to prolong your stay, there is accommodation to suit every taste: sea-view rooms (gaze at azure waves between fluttering curtains), dog-friendly rooms (no need to leave Fido at home), garden cottages (ideal for a small crowd), a self-catered bungalow (for exclusivity) and country-view rooms where you can immerse yourself in nature. Whichever you choose, you can dine well and drift off to sleep without a care.

Trencherman's tip: dinner at Talland Bay is a tasting experience: three exceptional courses are supplemented by canapés, amuse bouche, sourdough and whipped butter, pre-dessert, and coffee and petits fours.

Chef Glen Merriot | **3 course dinner from** £85
Seats 42 | **Bedrooms** 20 | **Room rate from** £220

109 The Longstore

Lively casual dining at Charlestown

Charlestown Road, Charlestown, Cornwall, PL25 3NJ **01726 68598**

thelongstore.co.uk

Each summer, picturesque Charlestown finds itself abuzz with visitors who, having seen it in the hit TV series *Poldark*, want to experience the historic harbour and grand tall ships for themselves. Happily, when they're ready to swap 18th-century romance for 21st-century dining there's lively hospitality waiting at The Longstore.

The industrial-chic restaurant is part of a next-gen family of foodie finds in the village – the portfolio includes a speciality coffee shop, wine store and pizzeria. At The Longstore, diners get to feast in a vibrant open-plan dining room that's been decked out by a team of local craftspeople who've mixed rustic and industrial styling to pleasingly casual effect.

Artistic flair is as prevalent in the kitchen where executive chefs William Spurgeon and Matthew Liddicoat create a crowd-pleasing menu. The pair excel at steaks (dry aged in-house) and seafood as much as upscale dishes like rosemary and garlic lamb rump with parmesan polenta and bitter leaf salsa verde.

To go uber casual, plump for the epic cheeseburger served with smoked cheddar beer sauce or get stuck into barbecued ribs with chipotle glaze. It's not all meaty treats and fresh fish however, as veggies and vegans are well catered for too.

For dessert, dig into revised classics such as the dark and stormy sticky toffee pud with rum-soaked raisins and vanilla ice cream.

Great cooking is complemented by an extensive wine and cocktail list which runs from not-to-be-messed-with stalwarts to newly invented concoctions.

Chefs William Spurgeon and Matthew Liddicoat | **3 course dinner from** £28.50 | **Seats** 100

110 The Barley Sheaf

Hyper-local pub dining near St Austell

Gorran Churchtown, St Austell, Cornwall, PL26 6HN **01726 843330**
thebarleysheafgorran.co.uk

Chef proprietor Tim Kendall took over The Barley Sheaf in February 2020 and, despite the difficult timing, has built a cracking reputation for delicious and well-executed dishes which perfectly reflect the surrounding seascape and countryside.

Decorated in earthy heritage tones with a slate floor and local artwork on the walls, this country inn is smart enough for occasion dining yet so easygoing that no-one would raise an eyebrow if you turned up with a four-legged friend in tow.

A rich abundance of produce from the farms and coast of Cornwall and the South West are reflected in the cooking, and Tim and team make a great effort to use fruit and veg grown by local parishioners.

The chef's crowd-pleasing pub classics – favourites include gourmet bangers and mash – sit alongside more adventurous fare such as wood pigeon with beetroot, black pudding, savoury granola and red chard.

Vegetarians and vegans aren't left out: dishes like miso-glazed aubergine with aubergine caviar, red pepper, pimento beans and a spicy Moroccan sauce are contemporary and innovative.

Tim also puts a local spin on trad puddings, including a white chocolate mousse dish crafted using Cornish fairings.

Suggested wine pairings and tipples by the glass make it easy to match your dish with something decent from a 40-strong wine list.

Chef Tim Kendall | **3 course dinner from** £30 | **Seats** 55

111 The Falmouth Arms

French classics in the countryside

Ladock, Cornwall, TR2 4PG **01726 882319**

falmoutharms.com

After almost a decade outside the county, Kevin Viner returned to Cornwall in 2019 to bring his classic French cooking to The Falmouth Arms at Ladock.

Kevin earned the first Michelin star for Cornwall in 1993 and retained the accolade at his restaurant PennyPots for nine years before moving on to pastures new. Many of the chefs who worked under him during that era (including Chris Eden of Gidleigh Park and Paul Ripely) have gone on to similar success.

Dining at The Falmouth Arms is an opportunity to revisit the kind of classic cooking that springboarded the South West restaurant scene's adventures in fine dining. Dishes such as twice-baked cheese soufflé, crab cocktail and duck à l'orange are exemplary in their execution and as timeless as they are nostalgic.

In winter, enjoy a pre-dinner drink by the fire in the cosy bar and browse the huge display of awards which Kevin has collected over the years. The wine list includes a few top picks from Cornish vineyards, including the delicious Camel Valley Sparkling Brut.

Four comfortable bedrooms above the pub offer a cosy night's slumber, while Kevin's classic breakfasts are worth staying over for.

Trencherman's tip: this welcoming dining pub makes a great gourmet pit stop on any touring trip through Cornwall.

Chef Kevin Viner | **3 course dinner from** £40
Seats 40 | **Bedrooms** 4 | **Room rate from** £100

salt

The essential ingredient for publishing,
marketing and design

saltmedia.co.uk

112 The Rising Sun

Truro's delicious dining pub

Mitchell Hill, Truro, Cornwall, TR1 1ED **01872 240003**
therisingsuntruro.co.uk

This cosy dining pub in Truro is a find for indulgent food, an intimate candlelit atmosphere, great beers and wines and barrels of bonhomie.

The Rising Sun chef patron Tom Hannon and partner Katie (who runs everything backstage – from drinks-list curation to event planning) combine a love of food culture and characterful wines and spirits with a passion for excellent Cornish produce at their charming edge-of-the-city find.

Sidestep the bustle of downtown Truro and take a five-minute stroll from the city centre to be embraced within the warm environs of this foodie favourite. Tom's creative, ever-evolving menus take the best of nearby land and sea; he crafts pleasing dishes from the likes of Cornish scallops, local pheasant breast and just-landed fish.

The wine list is just as thoughtfully designed and there's always something interesting to try (plus recommendations on what will pair best with each dish). The gin list and beers and ales are also noteworthy, so there's every reason to extend your pairing beyond the grape.

Kick off an evening at The Rising Sun with an aperitif by the fire (or in the courtyard garden on warm evenings), then settle in for a feast of rich and indulgent delights in the intimate restaurant.

Chef Tom Hannon | **3 course dinner from** £27 | **Seats** 40

113 The Longstore Lemon Street

Steak in the city

62 Lemon Street, Truro, Cornwall, TR1 2PN **01872 430000**
thelongstore.co.uk

Stylish city dining is served with a warm and welcoming Cornish vibe at this Lemon Street bar and grill.

The Longstore is a multi-functioning destination and as great for an express lunch with friends or after-work cocktails with colleagues as it is for leisurely three-course dining.

Soothing tones of potted-shrimp and sage, plus a glass atrium featuring gleaming handmade oyster chandeliers, add contemporary glamour to the recently refurbished Georgian townhouse.

As at its sister restaurant, The Longstore in Charlestown, the team specialise in seafood and steaks that deliver bold, vibrant flavours. Executive chefs Will Spurgeon and Matt Liddicoat, with the creative input of head chef Andrew Basso, create accessible menus with both small- and large-plate options.

Bijou bar bites like Cornish gilda pair well with cocktails such as the melon and elderflower spritz, while a starter of beef and blue cheese croquettes is as good for light grazing as it is an opener to mains of whole fish, seafood or marinated lamb rump.

However, it's the dry-aged steaks from local butchers that Longstore fans really rave about – choose from a list that runs from 18oz sirloins to 40oz tomahawks.

Many of the puddings feature a Duchy twist on a classic, such as pannacotta made from Cornish milk complemented by West Country strawberries and pink-peppercorn shortbread.

Saturday brunch and Sunday roast menus, plus a beer and wine curation overseen by drinks supremo Chris Jarrett, mean there's always something new to try.

Chef Andrew Basso | **3 course dinner from** £29.50 | **Seats** 80

114 The Watch House

Casual dining in St Mawes

1 The Square, St Mawes, Truro, Cornwall, TR2 5DJ **01326 270038**
watchhousestmawes.co.uk

'We sell seafood by the seashore' proudly asserts The Watch House team, and when the backdrop is the astonishingly beautiful seascape of St Mawes, it's an alluring proposition.

The smartly upmarket south coast village is blessed with more than its fair share of excellent dining options but, for joyfully casual cooking in a relaxed and attractive setting, this is your go-to.

Swing by straight off the beach for a lunch or supper of classic steak frites, the freshest dayboat catch or (star of the show) roasted shellfish platter care of Wing of St Mawes and Matthew Stevens Cornish Fish. There's no fuss or standing on ceremony here, just straight-up delicious local produce prepared by chef patron Will Gould and served in a relaxed, family-friendly environment.

Will's a huge proponent of supporting local artisan suppliers so you'll find delivery vans pulling up early each morning from top-notch producers such as Da Bara Bakery, Philip Warren Butchers and Harbour Brewing. Treleavens ice cream provides the sweet scoops while Rodda's delivers the clotted cream.

Those in the know visit for Porthilly rock oysters and the locals' favourite Keralan cod curry.

Trencherman's tip: fancy eating supper on the beach as the sun sets over the water? Get The Watch House's award-winning fish and chip supper to-go – just don't forget your picnic rug.

Chef Will Gould | **3 course dinner from** £35 | **Seats** 70

115 Hooked on the Rocks

Casual seafood feasts by the beach

Swanpool, Falmouth, Cornwall, TR11 5BG **01326 311886**

hookedontherocksfalmouth.com

Nothing quite captures the spirit of a Cornish summer than following a dip in its azure waters with a plate of lusciously fresh local seafood. Happily, that's just the experience to be savoured at Hooked on the Rocks, just yards from the shore of Swanpool Beach near Falmouth.

Visit to experience simple but scrumptious starters such as Falmouth Bay scallops with roe butter and seaweed pangrattato, and wild prawns with garlic butter, 'nduja, lime and fresh herbs. Mains of Falmouth Bay lobster or crab with garlic and herb butter, seaweed and garlic aioli, and crisp skinny fries satiate the appetite of any sandy-toed gourmet.

Fripperies and embellishments are minimal on this menu, allowing the briny delights to speak for themselves. It's a strategy that sees locals and holidaymakers flock to Hooked for sundowner seafood suppers – best enjoyed on the alfresco seating with a glass of Camel Valley Cornwall Brut or Sharp's Camel Valley Pilsner.

For more casual outdoor eats with equally impressive views, check out The Seahorse, the restaurant's converted horsebox which serves light bites such as Porthilly oysters with shallot mignonette and Tabasco, West Country mussels, and crab fries (shoelace chips topped with white crab meat, brown crab mayonnaise and chives).

Trencherman's tip: be sure to book in advance as this coastal spot is very popular.

Chef Jack Frame | **3 course dinner from** £40 | **Seats** 45 inside, 60 outside

116 The Harbourside Refuge Restaurant and Bar

Haven of hospitality

Mount Pleasant Road, Porthleven, Helston, Cornwall, TR13 9JS **01326 331758**
theharboursiderefuge.co.uk

Porthleven is legendary for its stormy weather and dramatic seas, so it's great to have a gourmet safe haven up your sleeve, where you can cosy up and enjoy delicious food prepared by Michael Caines' team.

Tucked into the port's pretty horseshoe cluster of pubs and restaurants, Harbourside Refuge lives up to its name as a snug hideaway in a gale. However, a rooftop terrace and alfresco tables make it an equally lovely destination when the weather is clement. Picture windows, too, make it the perfect spot for grazing on succulent seafood while gazing over the harbour's pale blues and bobbing boats.

All-day flexible and family-style menus make this welcoming restaurant an ideal destination for all manner of occasions:

from morning lattes and quick bites after walking the dog (downstairs is pooch friendly) to casual dinners with friends and blow-out celebrations.

Popular dishes such as rump of lamb and sirloin steak are crafted with utmost attention to detail while, for those pushing the boat out, the seven-course tasting menu with accompanying wine flight is a wonderful opportunity to sample Michael Caines' signature dishes.

Michael and head chef Jack Wilkinson see to it that dishes are crafted from the abundance of world-class ingredients grown and reared nearby. Fish is sourced from Cornish waters, making dishes such as wild cod with globe artichoke and watercress feel in perfect harmony with the glorious waterside setting.

Chefs Michael Caines and Jack Wilkinson | **3 course dinner from** £45 | **Seats** 100

Index

Index

Notes

For details of special dishes and drinks you've experienced at
Trencherman's restaurants